Copyright © 2003 Russ Kick

Published by The Disinformation Company Ltd.
163 Third Avenue, Suite 108, New York, NY 10003 / Tel.: +1.212.691.1605 / Fax: +1.212.473.8096
www.disinfo.com

Design & Layout: Rebecca Meek . thecreativeshop

First Printing October 2003

Library of Congress Control Number: 2003105111

ISBN 0-9713942-8-8

Printed in Mexico

Distributed in the USA and Canada by: Consortium Book Sales and Distribution
1045 Westgate Drive, Suite 90, St Paul, MN 55114 / Toll Free: +1.800.283.3572 / Local: +1.651.221.9035 / Fax: +1.651.221.0124 / www.cbsd.com

Distributed in the United Kingdom and Eire by: Turnaround Publisher Services Ltd.,
Unit 3, Olympia Trading Estate, Coburg Road, London, N22 6TZ / Tel.: +44.(0)20.8829.3000 / Fax: +44.(0)20.8881.5088 / www.turnaround-uk.com

Attention colleges and universities, corporations and other organizations:
Quantity discounts are available on bulk purchases of this book for educational training purposes, fund-raising, or gift-giving. Special books, booklets, or book excerpts can also be created to fit your specific needs. For information contact the Marketing Department of The Disinformation Company Ltd.

Disinformation is a registered trademark of The Disinformation Company Ltd.

50 THINGS YOU'RE NOT SUPPOSED TO KNOW

CONTENTS

CONTENTS

Certain parties don't want you to know certain facts. For example, if Bayer were proud that it introduced heroin to the world, wouldn't that fact be on the company's Website? After all, it was one of the most popular drugs of the twentieth century. The official corporate history mentions the release of aspirin in 1899 but not heroin during the previous year.

Do you think the Catholic Church wants you to know that Pope Pius II wrote an erotic book? True, the canonical *Catholic Encyclopedia* does mention the title in passing, but it demurely neglects to say anything about it.

Historians don't seem too happy about the fact that Winston Churchill decried an alleged worldwide Jewish conspiracy, so you won't read that very often. Likewise, the cannibalistic tendencies of the Virginia colonists and our close call with World War III are just too discomforting to be widely admitted.

My lady-love was an active feminist in the 1970s, yet she had never heard that the founding mothers of feminism opposed abortion. Small wonder, since their prolife views are almost never mentioned in biographies or documentaries. I was surprised when Richard Metzger, Disinformation's creative director, told me that Carl Sagan loved reefer. I guess the Drug Warriors won't be using the famous scientist as a poster child for the "evils" of pot.

The tobacco companies finally had to cop to lung cancer, but they still prefer that you remain ignorant of all the other health problems caused by smoking. You won't see "Causes blindness" or "Doubles risk of genital cancer" on the warning label. The beef industry sued Oprah Winfrey for discussing the possibility of mad cow disease in the US, so do you think that the dairy industry will be very happy when people find out that most milk starts out containing bovine leukemia virus?

Activists have been arrested for telling people about their full powers as jurors. Plans to nuke the Moon have been classified. The military successfully pressured a movie studio to change the name of a character in the flick *Black Hawk Down*; that particular commando is currently in the stockade for raping a child under twelve.

Certain parties don't want you to know certain facts. That's a fact. ▯

01
THE TEN COMMANDMENTS WE ALWAYS SEE AREN'T THE TEN COMMANDMENTS

First Amendment battles continue to rage across the US over the posting of the Ten Commandments in public places — courthouses, schools, parks, and pretty much anywhere else you can imagine. Christians argue that they're a part of our Western heritage that should be displayed as ubiquitously as traffic signs. Congressman Bob Barr hilariously suggested that the Columbine massacre wouldn't have happened if the Ten Commandments (also called the Decalogue) had been posted in the high school, and some government officials have directly, purposely disobeyed court rulings against the display of these ten directives supposedly handed down from on high.

Too bad they're all talking about the wrong rules.

Every Decalogue you see — from the 5,000-pound granite behemoth inside the Alabama State Judicial Building to the little wallet-cards sold at Christian bookstores — is bogus. Simply reading the Bible will prove this. Getting out your King James version, turn to Exodus 20:2-17. You'll see the familiar list of rules about having no other gods, honoring your parents, not killing or coveting, and so on. At this point, though, Moses is just repeating to the people what God told him on Mount Si'nai. These are not written down in any form.

Later, Moses goes back to the Mount, where God gives him two "tables of stone" with rules written on them (Exodus 31:18). But when Moses comes down the mountain lugging his load, he sees the people worshipping a statue of a calf, causing him to throw a tantrum and smash the tablets on the ground (Exodus 32:19).

In neither of these cases does the Bible refer to "commandments." In the first instance, they are "words" which "God spake," while the tablets contain "testimony." It is only when Moses goes back for new tablets that we see the phrase "ten commandments" (Exodus 34:28). In an interesting turn of events, the commandments on these tablets are significantly different than the ten rules Moses recited for the people, meaning that either Moses' memory is faulty or God changed his mind.

Thus, without further ado, we present to you the *real* "Ten Commandments" as handed down by the LORD unto Moses (and plainly listed in Exodus 34:13-28). We eagerly await all the new Decalogues, which will undoubtedly contain this correct version:

I. Thou shalt worship no other god.
II. Thou shalt make thee no molten gods.
III. The feast of unleavened bread thou shalt keep.
IV. Six days thou shalt work, but on the seventh day thou shalt rest.
V. Thou shalt observe the feast of weeks, of the firstfruits of wheat harvest, and the feast of ingathering at the year's end.
VI. Thrice in the year shall all your men children appear before the Lord God.
VII. Thou shalt not offer the blood of my sacrifice with leaven.
VIII. Neither shall the sacrifice of the feast of the passover be left unto the morning.
IX. The first of the firstfruits of thy land thou shalt bring unto the house of the LORD thy God.
X. Thou shalt not seethe a kid [ie, a young goat] in his mother's milk.

02
ONE OF THE POPES WROTE AN EROTIC BOOK

Before he was Pope Pius II, Aeneas Sylvius Piccolomini was a poet, scholar, diplomat, and rakehell. And an author. In fact, he wrote a bestseller. People in fifteenth-century Europe couldn't get enough of his Latin novella *Historia de duobus amantibus*. An article in a scholarly publication on literature claims that *Historia* "was undoubtedly one of the most read stories of the whole Renaissance." The Oxford edition gives a Cliff Notes version of the storyline: "*The Goodli History* tells of the illicit love of Euralius, a high official in the retinue of the [German] Emperor Sigismund, and Lucres, a married lady from Siena [Italy]."

It was probably written in 1444, but the earliest known printing is from Antwerp in 1488. By the turn of the century, 37 editions had been published. Somewhere around 1553, the short book appeared in English under the wonderfully old-school title *The Goodli History of the Moste Noble and Beautyfull Ladye Lucres of Scene in Tuskane, and of Her Louer Eurialus Verye Pleasaunt and Delectable vnto ye Reder*.

Despite the obvious historical interest of this archaic Vatican porn, it has never been translated into contemporary language. (The passages quoted below mark the first time that any of the book has appeared in modern English.)

The 1400s being what they were, the action is pretty tame by today's standards. At one point, Euralius scales a wall to be with Lucres: "When she saw her lover, she clasped him in her arms. There was embracing and kissing, and with full sail they followed their lusts and wearied Venus, now with Ceres, and now with Bacchus was refreshed." Loosely translated, that last part means that they shagged, then ate, then drank wine.

His Holiness describes the next time they hook up:

Thus talking to each other, they went into the bedroom, where they had such a night as we judge the two lovers Paris and Helen had after he had taken her away, and it was so pleasant that they thought Mars and Venus had never known such pleasure....

Her mouth, and now her eyes, and now her cheeks he kissed. Pulling down her clothes, he saw such beauty as he had never seen before. "I have found more, I believe," said Euralius, "than Acteon saw of Diana when she bathed in the fountain. What is more pleasant or more fair than these limbs?... O fair neck and pleasant breasts, is it you that I touch? Is it you that I have? Are you in my hands? O round limbs, O sweet body, do I have you in my arms?... O pleasant kisses, O dear embraces, O sweet bites, no man alive is happier than I am, or more blessed."...

He strained, and she strained, and when they were done they weren't weary. Like Athens, who rose from the ground stronger, soon after battle they were more desirous of war.

But Euralius isn't just a horndog. He waxes philosophical about love to Lucres' cousin-in-law:

You know that man is prone to love. Whether it is virtue or vice, it reigns everywhere. No heart of flesh hasn't sometime felt the pricks of love. You know that neither the wise Solomon nor the strong Sampson has escaped from this passion. Furthermore, the nature of a kindled heart and a foolish love is this: The more it is allowed, the more it burns, with nothing sooner healing this than the obtaining of the loved. There have been many, both in our time and that of our elders, whose foolish love has been the cause of cruel death. And many who, after sex and love vouchsafed, have stopped burning. Nothing is better when love has crept into your bones than to give in to the burning, for those who strive against the tempest often wreck, while those who drive with the storm escape.

Besides sex and wisdom, the story also contains a lot of humor, as when Lucres' husband borrows a horse from Euralius: "He says to himself, 'If you leap upon my horse, I shall do the same thing to your wife.'"

Popes just don't write books like that anymore! 🗘

03
THE CIA COMMITS OVER 100,000 SERIOUS CRIMES EACH YEAR

It's no big secret that the Central Intelligence Agency breaks the law. But just how often its does so is a shocker. A Congressional report reveals that the CIA's spooks "engage in highly illegal activities" at least *100,000* times each year (which breaks down to hundreds of crimes every day). Mind you, we aren't talking about run-of-the-mill illegal activities — these are "highly illegal activities" that "break extremely serious laws."

In 1996, the House of Representatives' Permanent Select Committee on Intelligence released a huge report entitled "IC21: The Intelligence Community in the 21st Century." Buried amid hundreds of pages is a single, devastating paragraph:

The CS [clandestine service] is the only part of the IC [intelligence community], indeed of the government, where hundreds of employees on a daily basis are directed to break extremely serious laws in countries around the world in the face of frequently sophisticated efforts by foreign governments to catch them. A safe estimate is that several hundred times every day (easily 100,000 times a year) DO [Directorate of Operations] officers engage in highly illegal activities (according to foreign law) that not only risk political embarrassment to the US but also endanger the freedom if not lives of the participating foreign nationals and, more than occasionally, of the clandestine officer himself.

Amazingly, there is no explanation, no follow-up. The report simply drops this bombshell and moves on as blithely as if it had just printed a grocery list.

One of the world's foremost experts on the CIA — John Kelly, who uncovered this revelation — notes that this is "the first official admission and definition of CIA covert operations as crimes." He goes on to say:

The report suggested that the CIA's crimes include murder and that "the targets of the CS [Clandestine Service] are increasingly international and transnational and a global presence is increasingly crucial to attack those targets." In other words, we are not talking about simply stealing secrets. We are talking about the CIA committing crimes against humanity with de facto impunity and congressional sanctioning.

Other government documents, including CIA reports, show that the CIA's crimes include terrorism, assassination, torture, and systematic violations of human rights. The documents also show that these crimes are part and parcel of deliberate CIA policy (the [congressional] report notes that CIA personnel are "directed" to commit crimes).

04
THE FIRST CIA AGENT TO DIE IN THE LINE
OF DUTY WAS DOUGLAS MACKIERNAN

As of the year 2000, 69 CIA agents had died in the line of duty. Of these, the identities of 40 remain classified. Former *Washington Post* and *Time* reporter Ted Gup spent three years tracking down information about these mysterious spooks who gave their lives for the Agency. (His resulting publication, *The Book of Honor*, names almost all of them.)

The first to die was Douglas Mackiernan. Undercover as a State Department diplomat, the US Army Air Corps Major worked in the capital of China's Xinjiang (Sinkiang) province, which Gup says "was widely regarded as the most remote and desolate consulate on earth." He went there in May 1947 to keep an eye on China's border with the Soviet Union and to monitor the Russkies' atomic tests.

In late September 1949, during the Communist takeover of China, Mackiernan left, but it was too late to use normal routes. Incredibly, he decided to go by foot during winter all the way to India, which would take him across a desert *and* the Himalayas. He, three White Russians, and a Fulbright scholar slogged the 1,000-mile trek in eight months. On April 29, 1950, they managed to reach the border of Tibet, but guards there thought the men were commies or bandits, and opened fire on them.

Hitting the ground, the bedraggled travelers waved a white flag, which stopped the gunfire. They slowly walked toward the border guards with their hands over their heads, but the Tibetans shot them, killing Mackiernan and two of the Russians. To add insult to injury, the guards cut the heads off the corpses. Their remains are buried at that spot.

With documents from the National Archives, Mackiernan's widow, and other sources, Gup pulled the CIA's first casualty out of the classified shadows. To this day, the Agency refuses to acknowledge Mackiernan's existence. ▢

05
AFTER 9/11, THE DEFENSE DEPARTMENT WANTED TO POISON AFGHANISTAN'S FOOD SUPPLY

One of the strangest things the media do is to bury huge revelations deep in the bowels of a larger story. A perfect example occurs in "10 Days in September," an epic eight-day series that ran in the *Washington Post*. In part six, Bob Woodward and Dan Balz are recounting the Bush Administration's activities on September 17, 2001, six days after the 9/11 attacks. Bush and National Security Advisor Condoleezza Rice have headed to the Pentagon to be briefed on action against Afghanistan by a two-star general from the Special Operation Command:

Rice and Frank Miller, the senior NSC staffer for defense, went with the president to the Pentagon. Before the briefing, Miller reviewed the classified slide presentation prepared for Bush and got a big surprise.

One slide about special operations in Afghanistan said: Thinking Outside the

Box — Poisoning Food Supply. Miller was shocked and showed it to Rice. The United States doesn't know how to do this, Miller reminded her, and we're not allowed. It would effectively be a chemical or biological attack — clearly banned by treaties that the United States had signed, including the 1972 Biological Weapons Convention.

Rice took the slide to Rumsfeld. "This slide is not going to be shown to the president of the United States," she said.

Rumsfeld agreed. "You're right," he said.

Pentagon officials said later that their own internal review had caught the offending slide and that it never would have been shown to the president or to Rumsfeld. ⟁

06
THE US GOVERNMENT LIES ABOUT THE NUMBER OF TERRORISM CONVICTIONS IT OBTAINS

Naturally enough, the Justice Department likes to trumpet convictions of terrorists. Besides garnering great publicity and allowing the citizenry to sleep snugly at night, this means more money for the department. The problem is that the numbers are a sham.

The story broke when the *Philadelphia Inquirer* examined convictions that the Justice Department said involved terrorism during the five year-period ending September 30, 2001. They found ludicrous examples of misclassification:

In one vivid example, an assistant US attorney in San Francisco asked US District Judge Marilyn H. Patel on Monday to stiffen a sentence against an Arizona man who got drunk on a United Airlines flight from Shanghai, repeatedly rang the call button, demanded more liquor, and put his hands on a flight attendant. Justice Department records show the case as "domestic terrorism."

In another case: "A tenant fighting eviction called his landlord, impersonated an FBI agent, and said the bureau did not want the tenant evicted. The landlord recognized the man's voice and called the real FBI."

Other "terrorist" incidents included prisoners rioting for better food, "the former court employee who shoved and threatened a judge," and "[s]even Chinese sailors [who] were convicted of taking over a Taiwanese fishing boat and sailing to the US territory of Guam, where they hoped to win political asylum."

After this chicanery was exposed, Republican Congressman Dan Burton asked the General Accounting Office — a nonpartisan governmental unit that investigates matters for Congress — to look into the Justice Department's claims of terrorist convictions. Sure enough, the GAO reported that the situation isn't nearly as rosy as we've been told.

In the year after 9/11 — from September 30, 2001, to that date the following year — the Justice Department maintained that 288 terrorists had been convicted in the US of their heinous crimes. But the GAO found that at least 132 of these cases (approximately 42 percent) had *nothing* to do with terrorism. Because of the GAO's methodology, it didn't verify every one of the remaining 156 convictions, so it refers to their accuracy as "questionable."

The deception is even worse when you zoom in on the cases classified as "international terrorism," which are the most headline-grabbing of all. Out of 174 such convictions, 131 (an amazing 75 percent) weren't really about terror.

After all of this humiliation, the Justice Department must've cleaned up its act, right? That's what it told the *Philadelphia Inquirer*. Well, the paper did a follow-up on "terrorism" cases for the first two months of 2003. Out of the 56 federal cases supposedly involving terrorism, at least 41 were bogus. Eight of them involved Puerto Ricans protesting the Navy's use of Vieques as a bombing range. The prosecutor who handled these cases says she doesn't know why they were classified as terrorism. Similarly, 28 Latinos were arrested for working at airports with phony ID, and a spokesman for the US Attorney says they weren't even suspected of being involved in terrorism. The most ridiculous example: "A Middle Eastern man indicted in Detroit for allegedly passing bad checks who has the same name as a Hezbollah leader." ▯

07
THE US IS PLANNING TO *PROVOKE* TERRORIST ATTACKS

Perhaps the government won't need to inflate its terrorism-arrest stats after it implements the Defense Science Board's recommendation. This influential committee inside the Pentagon has proposed a terrifying way to fight evil-doers: Goad them into making terrorist attacks. Yes, you read correctly. Instead of waiting for a plot to be hatched and possibly executed, go out and *make* it happen.

In summer 2002, the Defense Science Board outlined all kinds of ways to fight the war on terrorism around the world. The scariest suggestion involves the creation of a new 100-man, $100-million team called the Proactive Pre-emptive Operations Group, or P2OG.

This combination of elite special forces soldiers and intelligence agents will have "an entirely new capability to proactively, pre-emptively provoke responses from adversary/terrorist groups," according to the DSB's report.

Just how the P2OG will "provoke" terrorists into action is not specified, at least in the unclassified portions of the report. United Press International — which apparently has access to the full, classified version of the report — says that techniques could include "stealing their money or tricking them with fake communications." The *Moscow Times* offers further possibilities, such as killing family members and infiltrating the groups with provocateurs, who will suggest and even direct terrorist strikes.

Once the terrorists have been provoked, what then? UPI says that by taking action, the terrorists would be "exposing themselves to 'quick-response' attacks by US forces." In other words, the plan is to hit the hornet's nest with a stick, while waiting nearby with a can of bug spray. The flaws in this approach are obvious. Although not spelled out in the UPI article or the report itself, the idea seems to be that the P2OG will cause terrorists to make an attack but supposedly stop them right before the attack actually occurs. Will the P2OG always be able to prevent terrorism it creates from taking place? Will it always be able to "neutralize" all of the terrorists during that crucial window after a plan has been put into motion but before it's been carried out? I wouldn't want to bet lives on it. But that's exactly what's happening.

Whenever any future terrorist attack occurs — an embassy is truck-bombed, a nightclub is blown to smithereens, prominent buildings are hit with hijacked passenger jets — we'll never be 100 percent sure that this wasn't an operation the P2OG provoked but then was unable to stop in time. ▢

08
THE US AND SOVIET UNION CONSIDERED DETONATING NUCLEAR BOMBS ON THE MOON

You'd be forgiven for thinking that this is an unused scene from *Dr. Strangelove*, but the United States and the Soviet Union have seriously considered exploding atomic bombs on the Moon.

It was the late 1950s, and the Cold War was extremely chilly. Someone in the US government got the bright idea of nuking the Moon, and in 1958 the Air Force Special Weapons Center spearheaded the project (labeled A119, "A Study of Lunar Research Flights").

The idea was to shock and awe the Soviet Union, and everybody else, with a massive display of American nuclear might. What better demonstration than an atomic explosion on our closest celestial neighbor? According to the project's reports, the flash would've been visible to the naked eye on Earth. (It's been suggested that another motivation may have been to use the Moon as a test range, thus avoiding the problems with irradiating our home planet.)

Carl Sagan was among the scientists lending his intellectual muscle to this hare-brained scheme. The project's leader was physicist Leonard Reiffel, who said: "I made it clear at the time there would be a huge cost to science of destroying a pristine lunar environment, but the US Air Force were mainly concerned about how the nuclear explosion would play on earth."

When a reporter for Reuters asked him what had happened to Project A119, Reiffel replied, "After the final report in early- to mid-1959, it simply went away, as things sometimes do in the world of classified activities."

Astoundingly, this wasn't the only time that a nuclear strike on the Moon was contemplated. Science reporter Keay Davidson reveals that "in 1956, W.W. Kellogg of RAND Corporation considered the possibility of launching an atomic bomb to the Moon." In 1957, NASA's Jet Propulsion Laboratory put forth Project Red Socks, the first serious proposal to send spacecraft to the Moon. One of its lesser suggestions was to nuke the Moon in order to send lunar rocks hurtling back to Earth, where they could be collected and studied. The following year, the leading American astronomer of the time, Gerard Kuiper, coauthored a memo which considered the scientific advantages of nuking the Moon. The creator of the hydrogen bomb, physicist Edward Teller, similarly mused about dropping atomic bombs on the Moon in order to study the seismic waves they would create.

The Soviet Union got in on the act, also in the late 1950s. Project E-4 would've used a probe armed with an A-bomb to blast the Moon, apparently as a display of one-upmanship. The idea reached the stage of a full-scale model but was aborted for fear of the probe falling back to Earth. ▢

09
TWO ATOMIC BOMBS WERE DROPPED ON NORTH CAROLINA

Fortunately, no atomic bombs were dropped on the Moon, but the same can't be said of North Carolina. The Tar Heel State's brush with nuclear catastrophe came on January 24, 1961, about half past midnight. A B-52 with two nukes on-board was cruising the skies near Goldsboro and Faro when its right wing leaked fuel and exploded. The jet disintegrated. Five crewmen survived, while three died.

The two MARK 39 thermonuclear bombs disengaged from the jet. Each one had a yield of two to four megatons (reports vary), up to 250 times as powerful as the bomb that decimated

Hiroshima. The parachute opened on one of them, and it drifted to the earth relatively gently. But the parachute failed to open on the other, so it plowed into a marshy patch of land owned by a farmer.

The nuke with the parachute was recovered easily. However, its twin proved much more difficult to retrieve. Because of the swampiness of the area, workers were able to drag out only part of the bomb. One of its most crucial components — the "secondary," which contains nuclear material — is still in the ground, probably around 150 feet down.

The federal government bought rights to this swatch of land to prevent any owners from digging more than five feet under the surface. To this day, state regulators test the radiation levels of the ground water in the area every year. The head of the North Carolina Division of Radiation Protection has said that they've found only normal levels but that "there is still an open question as to whether a hazard exists."

The big question is whether or not North Carolina's own Fat Man and Little Boy could've actually detonated. Due to the technicalities of nuclear weapons — and the ambiguous nature of the terms "unarmed," "armed," and "partially armed" — it's hard to give a definitive answer. We do know this: The Defense Department said that the ill-fated B-52 was part of a program (since discontinued) that continuously kept nuclear bombs in the air, ready for dropping. So, the answer is yes, that jet was fully capable of unleashing its A-bombs in completely armed mode, with all that this implies — mushroom clouds, vaporized people, dangerous radiation levels for decades, etc.

According to the late Chuck Hansen — one of the world's leading authorities on nuclear weapons — the pilot of the B-52 would've had to throw a switch to arm the bombs. Since he didn't, the bombs couldn't have gone off. Hansen mentions the possibility that the switch could've been activated while the jet was breaking apart and exploding. Luckily this didn't happen, but it was a possibility.

That switch apparently was the only thing that stopped the bombs from turning part of North Carolina into toast. The government's own reports show that for both bombs, *three* of the four arming devices had activated. Former Secretary of Defense Robert McNamara further corroborated this during a press conference, saying that the nukes "went through all but one" of the necessary steps.

Hansen told college students researching this near-miss:

This was a very dangerous incident and I suspect that steps were taken afterwards to prevent any repetition of it. I do not now know of any other weapon accident that came this close to a full-scale nuclear detonation (which is not to say that any such incident did not occur later). ⌂

10
WORLD WAR III ALMOST STARTED IN 1995

What were you doing on January 25, 1995? Whatever it was, it was almost the last thing you ever did. On that day, the world came within minutes of a nuclear war between the US and Russia.

Norway and the United States had launched a research rocket (for charting the Arctic) from a Norwegian island. Following standard protocol, Norway had alerted Russia in advance about the firing, but the message never made its way to the right people. In the middle of the night, Russian radar detected what looked like a nuclear missile launched toward Moscow from a US submarine.

The military immediately called President Boris Yeltsin, awakening him with the news that the country appeared to be under attack (no word on whether Yeltsin had been in a vodka-induced drunken slumber). The groggy president, for the first time ever, activated the infamous black suitcase that contains the codes for launching nuclear missiles. He had just a few minutes to decide whether to launch any or all of the country's 2,000 hair-trigger nukes at the US.

Luckily for the entire world, while Yeltsin was conferring with his highest advisors, Russia's radar showed that the missile was headed out to sea. The red alert was cancelled. World War III was averted.

What makes this even more nerve-racking is that Russia's early-warning systems are in much worse shape now than they were in '95. The Institute of Electrical and Electronic Engineers explains that while Russia needs 21 satellites to have a complete, fully-redundant network capable of accurately detecting missile launches, as of 1999 they have only three. Heaven help us if some Russian bureaucrat again forgets to tell the command and control center that a nearby country is launching a research rocket. ⌗

11
THE KOREAN WAR NEVER ENDED

Better not tell Hawkeye Pierce and the rest of the gang from *M*A*S*H*, but the Korean War is technically still happening. This comes to us from no less an authority than Howard S. Levie, the man who drafted the Korean Armistice Agreement. At the time, this law professor was a captain in the Office of the Judge Advocate General (JAG). He explains:

An armistice is not a peace treaty. While its main objective is to bring about a cease-fire, a halt to hostilities, that halt may be indefinite or for a specified period of time only. An armistice agreement does not terminate the state of war between the belligerents. A state of war continues to exist with all of its implications for the belligerents and for the neutrals.

The Korean Armistice itself even specifies that it is only a stop-gap measure "until a final peaceful settlement is achieved." To date, this settlement — otherwise known as a peace treaty — has never occurred. One attempt was made, at the Geneva Convention of 1954, but nothing came of it.

Interestingly, the Armistice wasn't signed at all by South Korea but rather by the head honchos in the United Nations Command, North Korea's army, and China's army. It should also be noted that the conflict in Korea wasn't technically a "war," because — like so many other post-WWII hostilities — there was no formal declaration of war. As *The Korean War: An Encyclopedia* trenchantly observes: "Since the war had never been declared, it was fitting that there should be no official ending, merely a suspension of hostilities."

North Korea has more than once denounced the Armistice, threatening to press the "play" button on the long-paused Korean War. Most recently, in February 2003, Kim Jong-il's government said that because of repeated US violations, the Armistice is merely "a blank piece of paper without any effect or significance."

12
AGENT ORANGE WAS USED IN KOREA

"Agent Orange" is practically synonymous with the Vietnam War. The Dow Chemical defoliant was used to de-junglize large areas, exposing enemy troops, supplies, and infiltrators. It has been linked, though never definitively, to a number of nasty health problems such as Hodgkin's disease and adult-onset diabetes, plus spina bifida in offspring. The Veterans Administration compensates sick veterans who were exposed in Vietnam.

But it turns out that 'Nam wasn't the only place to get doused with this super-herbicide. From April 1968 to July 1969, 21,000 gallons of Agent Orange were sprayed along a strip of land abutting the southern border of the Demilitarized Zone between the two Koreas. During that time period, around 80,000 US military personnel served in South Korea, although not all of them would've been in the vicinity of the DMZ. The VA contradicts itself regarding who did the spraying, claiming at one point that it was South Korea but saying at another that the Department of Defense did it.

In September 2000, the VA quietly sent letters to veterans who served in Korea during the spraying, letting them know that they may have been dosed with Agent Orange. Since these letters were sent over 30 years after the exposure, the Pentagon must've just found out about it, right? Actually, even if you buy the story that the South Koreans were responsible, the US military knew about the spraying at the time it happened but kept quiet about it for decades. It was only when news reports began citing declassified documents in 1999 that the government decided to do something.

Possibly exposed vets can get tested for free by the Veterans Administration. The catch is, if they're sick with Hodgkin's or some other horrible disease, they — unlike their Vietnam compatriots — aren't eligible for compensation or additional health care. However, for their agony, Korean vets will receive a free newsletter, the same one that Vietnam vets get. ▢

13
KENT STATE WASN'T THE ONLY — OR EVEN THE FIRST — MASSACRE OF COLLEGE STUDENTS DURING THE VIETNAM ERA

It's one of the defining moments of the Vietnam era and, more than that, twentieth-century US history in general. On May 4, 1970, the Ohio National Guard opened fire on unarmed Kent State University students protesting the war. Four were killed, eight were wounded, and another was left paralyzed. It's so ingrained in the country's psyche that it even appears in American history textbooks, and the anniversary is noted each year by the major media.

Yet this wasn't the only time the authorities slaughtered unarmed college kids during this time period. It happened on at least two other occasions, which have been almost completely forgotten.

A mere ten days after the Kent State massacre, students at the historically black Jackson State University in Mississippi were protesting not only the Vietnam War and the recent killings at Kent, but racism as well. On the night of May 14, 1970, during the protests, a small riot broke out when a false rumor swept the campus: The black mayor of Fayette, Mississippi, was said to have been assassinated. As at Kent State, some students or provocateurs threw bricks and stones and set fires. Firefighters trying to put out a blaze in a men's dorm were hassled by an angry crowd, so they called for police protection. The campus was cordoned off.

Jackson State's Website devoted to the incident says: "Seventy-five city policemen and Mississippi State Police officers armed with carbines, submachine guns, shotguns, service revolvers and some personal weapons, responded to the call." After the fire had been extinguished, the heavily armed cops marched down the street, herding students towards a women's dorm. As the Website notes: "No one seems to know why."

Seventy-five to 100 students were pushed back until they were in front of the dorm, where they began yelling and throwing things at the police. "Accounts disagree as to what happened next. Some students said the police advanced in a line, warned them, then opened fire. Others said the police abruptly opened fire on the crowd and the dormitory. Other witnesses reported that the students were under the control of a campus security officer when the police opened fire. Police claimed they spotted a powder flare in the Alexander West Hall third floor stairwell window and opened fire in self-defense on the dormitory only. Two local television news reporters present at the shooting agreed that a shot was fired, but were uncertain of the direction. A radio reporter claimed to have seen an arm and a pistol extending from a dormitory window."

Two people — both outside the dorm — were killed in over 30 seconds of sustained gunfire from the cops. Jackson student Phillip Lafayette Gibbs was shot in the head, and a bystander — high-school senior James Earl Green — took it in the chest. A dozen students were nonfatally shot, and many more were injured by flying glass. Over 460 rounds had hit the dorm. No member of law enforcement was injured.

After the carnage, Inspector "Goon" Jones radioed the dispatcher, saying that "nigger students" had been killed. When the dispatcher asked him about the injured, he said: "I think there are about three more nigger males there…. There were two nigger gals — two more nigger gals from over there shot in the arm, I believe."

Even less known is the Orangeburg massacre, which took place two years earlier. Students at South Carolina State University in Orangeburg — joined by students from another black college, Claflin University — were protesting the failure of the town's only bowling alley to racially integrate. February 8, 1968, was the fourth night of demonstrations, and students had lit a bonfire on campus. Police doused it, but a second one was started. When the cops tried to extinguish this one, the crowd — in a scene to be replayed at Kent and Jackson — started throwing things at them. One highway patrolmen fired warning shots into the air, and all hell broke loose as the assembled police opened fire on the unarmed crowd.

After a barrage of weapons-fire, three people were dead — eighteen-year-olds Henry Smith and Samuel Hammond, and high-school student Delano Middleton. Twenty-seven other demonstrators were wounded. The vast majority of them had been shot in the back as they ran away.

South Carolina's Governor praised the police for their handling on the situation, giving all of them promotions. Nine patrolmen were eventually tried on federal charges, and all were acquitted. It was only 33 years later — on the 2001 anniversary of the carnage — that a Governor of the state admitted the heinous nature of what happened that night. Governor Jim Hodges said, "We deeply regret" the mass-shooting, but he stopped short of apologizing for it. ▢

ILLUSTRATED SUNDAY HERALD, FEBRUARY 8, 1920.   Page 1.

ZIONISM versus BOLSHEVISM.
A STRUGGLE FOR THE SOUL OF THE JEWISH PEOPLE.
By the Rt. Hon. WINSTON S. CHURCHILL.

Like Henry Ford, Britain's larger-than-life wartime Prime Minister, Winston Churchill, believed that a group of "international Jews" was striving to take over the world. On February 8, 1920, the *Illustrated Sunday Herald* (published in London) ran an article by Churchill. Its title: "Zionism Versus Bolshevism: A Struggle for the Soul of the Jewish People." At the time, Winnie was Secretary of State for War and Air and had already been a prominent Member of Parliament.

Churchill didn't slam all Jews; rather, he painted them as a people of two extremes. "The conflict between good and evil which proceeds unceasingly in the breast of man nowhere reaches such an intensity as in the Jewish race. The dual nature of mankind is nowhere more strongly or more terribly exemplified…. It would almost seem as if the gospel of Christ and the gospel of Antichrist were destined to originate among the same people; and that this mystic and mysterious race had been chosen for the supreme manifestations, both of the divine and the diabolical."

He identifies three strains of political thought among the world's Jews: Nationalism, in which a

Jewish person identifies first and foremost with the country in which he or she lives. Zionism, in which a Jewish person wants a country specifically for Jews (Israel would be formed 28 years after Winnie's essay). These are both honorable, says Churchill, unlike the third option — the terrorism and atheistic communism of "International Jews." He writes:

International Jews
In violent opposition to all this sphere of Jewish effort rise the schemes of the International Jews. The adherents of this sinister confederacy are mostly men reared up among the unhappy populations of countries where Jews are persecuted on account of their race. Most, if not all, of them have forsaken the faith of their forefathers, and divorced from their minds all spiritual hopes of the next world. This movement among the Jews is not new. From the days of Spartacus-Weishaupt to those of Karl Marx, and down to Trotsky (Russia), Bela Kun (Hungary), Rosa Luxembourg (Germany), and Emma Goldman (United States), this world-wide conspiracy for the overthrow of civilization and for the reconstitution of society on the basis of arrested development, of envious malevolence, and impossible equality, has been steadily growing. It played, as a modern writer, Mrs. Webster, has so ably shown, a definitely recognizable part in the tragedy of the French Revolution. It has been the mainspring of every subversive movement during the Nineteenth Century; and now at last this band of extraordinary personalities from the underworld of the great cities of Europe and America have gripped the Russian people by the hair of their heads and have become practically the undisputed masters of that enormous empire.

Terrorist Jews

There is no need to exaggerate the part played in the creation of Bolshevism and in the actual bringing about of the Russian Revolution, by these international and for the most part atheistical Jews, it is certainly a very great one; it probably outweighs all others. With the notable exception of Lenin, the majority of the leading figures are Jews. Moreover, the principal inspiration and driving power comes from the Jewish leaders. Thus Tchitcherin, a pure Russian, is eclipsed by his nominal subordinate Litvinoff, and the influence of Russians like Bukharin or Lunacharski cannot be compared with the power of Trotsky, or of Zinovieff, the Dictator of the Red Citadel (Petrograd) or of Krassin or Radek — all Jews. In the Soviet institutions the predominance of Jews is even more astonishing. And the prominent, if not indeed the principal, part in the system of terrorism applied by the Extraordinary Commissions for Combating Counter-Revolution has been taken by Jews, and in some notable cases by Jewesses. The same evil prominence was obtained by Jews in the brief period of terror during which Bela Kun ruled in Hungary. The same phenomenon has been presented in Germany (especially in Bavaria), so far as this madness has been allowed to prey upon the temporary prostration of the German people. Although in all these countries there are many non-Jews every whit as bad as the worst of the Jewish revolutionaries, the part played by the latter in proportion to their numbers in the population is astonishing.

Naturally, Churchill's admirers aren't exactly proud of this essay, which has led some of them to question its authenticity. However, the leading Churchill bibliographer, Frederick Woods, has pronounced the article genuine, listing it in his authoritative *A Bibliography of the Works of Sir Winston Churchill.* ⌂

15
THE AUSCHWITZ TATTOO WAS ORIGINALLY AN IBM CODE NUMBER

The tattooed numbers on the forearms of people held and killed in Nazi concentration camps have become a chilling symbol of hatred. Victims were stamped with the indelible number in a dehumanizing effort to keep track of them like widgets in the supply chain.

These numbers obviously weren't chosen at random. They were part of a coded system, with each number tracked as the unlucky person who bore it was moved through the system.

Edwin Black made headlines in 2001 when his painstakingly researched book, *IBM and the Holocaust*, showed that IBM machines were used to automate the "Final Solution" and the jackbooted takeover of Europe. Worse, he showed that the top levels of the company either knew or willfully turned a blind eye.

A year and a half after that book gave Big Blue a black eye, the author made more startling discoveries. IBM equipment was on-site at the Auschwitz concentration camp. Furthermore:

Thanks to the new discoveries, researchers can now trace how Hollerith numbers

assigned to inmates evolved into the horrific tattooed numbers so symbolic of the Nazi era. (Herman Hollerith was the German American who first automated US census information in the late 19th century and founded the company that became IBM. Hollerith's name became synonymous with the machines and the Nazi "departments" that operated them.) In one case, records show, a timber merchant from Bendzin, Poland, arrived at Auschwitz in August 1943 and was assigned a characteristic five-digit IBM Hollerith number, 44673. The number was part of a custom punch-card system devised by IBM to track prisoners in all Nazi concentration camps, including the slave labor at Auschwitz. Later in the summer of 1943, the Polish timber merchant's same five-digit Hollerith number, 44673, was tattooed on his forearm. Eventually, during the summer of 1943, all non-Germans at Auschwitz were similarly tattooed.

The Hollerith numbering system was soon scrapped at Auschwitz because so many inmates died. Eventually, the Nazis developed their own haphazard system. ⌓

16
ADOLPH HITLER'S BLOOD RELATIVES ARE ALIVE AND WELL IN NEW YORK STATE

Adolph Hitler never had kids, so we tend to take for granted the idea that no one alive is closely related to him. But historians have long known that he had a nephew who was born in Britain and moved to the United States. Alois Hitler, Jr., was Adolph's older half-brother (their common parent was Alois Sr.). Alois Jr. — a waiter in Dublin — married an Irish woman, and, after moving to Liverpool, they had a son, William Patrick Hitler.

Pat, as he was called, moved to Germany as a young adult to take advantage of his uncle's rising political stature, but Adolph just gave him minor jobs and kept him out of the limelight. After being subtly threatened by Rudolph Hess to become a German citizen, and having gotten tired of being dissed by Adolph, Pat came to America in 1939 and went on a lecture tour around the US, denouncing his uncle. (For his part, Adolph referred to his nephew as "loathsome.") While World War II was raging, Pat joined the US Navy, so he could fight against Uncle Adolph. Afterwards, he changed his last name, and this is where the trail goes cold.

That is, until US-based British reporter David Gardner was assigned to track down and interview William Patrick. Originally given two weeks to file the story, Gardner realized that finding Hitler's long-lost nephew was tougher than it first appeared. He worked on the story during his spare time for several years, unearthing old news clippings, filing requests for government documents, interviewing possible relatives, and chasing a lot of dead ends.

He finally discovered that William Patrick had ended up in a small town in Long Island, New York. Pat had died in 1987, but Gardner showed up unannounced on the doorstep of his widow, Phyllis, who confirmed that her late husband was Adolph Hitler's nephew. She also mentioned that she and Pat had sons, but she quickly clammed up and asked Gardner to leave. The two never spoke again.

After more legwork, Gardner found that Pat and Phyllis produced four children, all sons. The eldest, born in 1949, is named Alexander Adolph. (Just why Pat would name his firstborn after his detested uncle is one of many mysteries still surrounding the Hitler kin.) Then came Louis in 1951, Howard (1957), and Brian (1965). Howard — a fraud investigator for the IRS — died in a car crash in 1989, and Louis and Brian continue to run a landscaping business in the small New York community. Alex lives in a larger Long Island city. He twice spoke to Gardner but didn't reveal very much, saying that the family's ancestry is "a pain in the ass." Alex said that his brothers made a pact never to have children, in order to spare their progeny the burden of being related to a monster. He denied having made such a vow himself, despite the fact that he is still childless.

Gardner sums it up: "Although there are some distant relations living equally quiet lives in Austria, the three American sons are the only descendants of the paternal line of the family. They are, truly, the last of the Hitlers."

17
AROUND ONE QUARTER OF "WITCHES" WERE MEN

The word "witch" has become synonymous with "woman accused of working magic," and the consensus tells us that the witch trials in Europe and Colonial America were simply a war against women (ie, "gendercide"). Most popular works on the subject ignore the men who were accused and executed for supposedly practicing witchcraft. Academic works that don't omit male witches usually explain them away, as if they were just a few special cases that don't really count.

Into this gap step Andrew Gow, an associate professor of history at the University of Alberta, and one of his grad students, Lara Apps. Their book *Male Witches in Early Modern Europe* scours the literature and finds that, of the 110,000 people tried for witchcraft and the 60,000 executed from 1450 to 1750, somewhere between 20 to 25 percent were men.

This is an average across Europe, the British Isles, and the American Colonies; the gender ratios vary widely from place to place. The lowest percentages of males were persecuted in the Basel region of Switzerland (5 percent) and in Hungary (10 percent). Places that hovered around the 50/50 mark were Finland (49 percent) and Burgundy (52 percent). Men were the clear majority of "witches" in Estonia (60 percent) and Norway (73 percent). During Iceland's witch craze, from 1625 to 1685, an amazing 110 out of 120 "witches" were men, for a percentage of 92. As for America, almost a third of those executed during the infamous Salem witch trials (six out of nineteen) were men.

Besides bringing these numbers to light, professor Gow and pupil Apps present serious challenges to the attempts to erase male witches from the picture. For example, some writers claim that the men were caught up in the hysteria solely because they were related to accused women. In this scenario, the men were only "secondary targets" ("collateral damage," perhaps?). But in numerous instances men were persecuted by themselves. In other cases, a woman became a secondary target *after* her husband had been singled out as a witch.

Although women were the overall majority of victims, the "burning times" were pretty rough for men, too. ⌁

18
THE VIRGINIA COLONISTS PRACTICED CANNIBALISM

During the harsh winter of 1609-1610, British subjects in the famous colony of Jamestown, Virginia, ate their dead and their shit. This fact doesn't make it into very many US history textbooks, and the state's official Website apparently forgot to mention it in their history section.

When you think about it rationally, this fact should be a part of mainstream history. After all, it demonstrates the strong will to survive among the colonists. It shows the mind-boggling hardships they endured and overcame. Yet the taboo against eating these two items is so over-powering that this episode can't be mentioned in conventional history.

Luckily, an unconventional historian, Howard Zinn, revealed this fact in his classic *A People's History of the United States*. Food was so nonexistent during that winter, only 60 out of 500 colonists survived. A government document from that time gives the gruesome details:

Driven thru insufferable hunger to eat those things which nature most abhorred, the flesh and excrements of man as well of our own nation as of an Indian, digged by some out of his grave after he had lain buried three days and wholly devoured him; others, envying the better state of body of any whom hunger has not yet so much wasted as their own, lay wait and threatened to kill and eat them; one among them slew his wife as she slept in his bosom, cut her in pieces, salted her and fed upon her till he had clean devoured all parts saving her head. ⌑

19
MANY OF THE PIONEERING FEMINISTS OPPOSED ABORTION

The idea that feminism equals the right to an abortion has become so ingrained that it seems ludicrous to think otherwise. "Prolife feminism" appears to be an inherent contradiction in terms. Yet more than 20 founding mothers of the feminist movement — who helped secure women's rights to vote, to own property, to use contraception, to divorce abusive husbands — were adamantly opposed to abortion.

The most famous nineteenth-century feminist — Susan B. Anthony, she of the ill-fated dollar coin — referred to abortion as "the horrible crime of child-murder." And that's just for starters. She also called it "infanticide," "this most monstrous crime," "evil," and a "dreadful deed." Surprisingly, given that unsparing language, she didn't believe that it should be made illegal. Responding to an article in which a man called for the outlawing of abortion, Anthony writes: "Much as I deplore the horrible crime of child-murder, earnestly as I desire its suppression, I cannot believe with the writer of the above-mentioned article, that such a law would have the desired effect. It seems to be only mowing off the top of the noxious weed, while the root remains."

The root, she believed, was the horrible way in which women (and children) were treated. As summed up in the book *Prolife Feminism*, these pioneering women felt that "abortion was the product of a social system that compelled women to remain ignorant about their bodies, that enabled men to dominate them sexually without taking responsibility for the consequences, that denied women support during and after the resulting pregnancies, and that placed far more value on a child's 'legitimacy' than on his or her life and well-being."

Indeed, while Anthony gave women a lot of grief for ending a pregnancy, she reserved the most vitriol for the men who knocked them up:

> **Guilty? Yes, no matter what the motive, love of ease, or a desire to save from suffering the unborn innocent, the woman is awfully guilty who commits the deed. It will burden her conscience in life, it will burden her soul in death; but oh! thrice guilty is he who, for selfish gratification, heedless of her prayers, indifferent to her fate, drove her to the desperation which impelled her to her crime.**

Elizabeth Cady Stanton, Anthony's best friend for life, resented society's dictate that all women must become mothers. Yet she also thought that "maternity is grand," but it must be on the woman's own terms. Despite this, she railed against abortion. Like her pal, she referred to abortions as "murder," "a crying evil," "abominations," and "revolting outrages against the laws of nature and our common humanity." Also like Anthony, Stanton laid the blame for abortion at the feet of men.

Dr. Elizabeth Blackwell, lionized as the first US woman to become a medical doctor (in 1849), wrote in her diary:

The gross perversion and destruction of motherhood by the abortionist filled me with indignation, and awakened active antagonism. That the honorable term "female physician" should be exclusively applied to those women who carried on this shocking trade seemed to me a horror. It was an utter degradation of what might and should become a noble position for women.

Another prolife feminist was Victoria Woodhull, best known for being the first female candidate for US President (way back in 1870). Radical even by early feminist standards, she and her sister, Tennessee Claflin, declared that children had rights which began at conception. Their essay "The Slaughter of the Innocents" first discusses the abominable death rate of children under five, then turns its sights on abortion:

We are aware that many women attempt to excuse themselves for procuring abortions, upon the ground that it is not murder. But the fact of resort to so weak an argument only shows the more palpably that they fully realize the enormity of the crime. Is it not equally destroying the would-be future oak, to crush the sprout before it pushes its head above the sod, as it is to cut down the sapling, or cut down the tree? Is it not equally to destroy life, to crush it in its very germ, and to take it when the germ has evolved to any given point in its line of development? Let those who can see any difference regarding the time when life, once begun, is taken, console themselves that they are not murderers having been abortionists. 🖸

20
BLACK PEOPLE SERVED IN THE CONFEDERATE ARMY

Like "prolife feminist," the phrase "black Confederate" seems like an oxymoron. But the record shows that many slaves and free blacks were a part of the South's military during the US Civil War.

None other than abolitionist Frederick Douglass, a former slave and one of the most prominent African Americans in history, declared:

There are at present moment [autumn 1861], many colored men in the Confederate Army doing duty not only as cooks, servants, and laborers, but as real soldiers, having musket on their shoulders and bullets in their pockets, ready to shoot down loyal troops and do all that soldiers may do to destroy the Federal government and build up that of the traitors and rebels.

In *Black Confederates and Afro-Yankees in Civil War Virginia*, Professor Ervin L. Jordan, Jr., writes:

Numerous black Virginians served with Confederate forces as soldiers, sailors, teamsters, spies, and hospital personnel.... I know of black Confederate sharpshooters who saw combat during the 1862 Seven Days Campaign and [of] the existence of black companies [which] organized and drilled in Richmond in March-April 1865. Integrated companies of black and white hospital workers fought against the Union army in the Petersburg trenches during March 1865. There were

several recruitment campaigns and charity balls held in Virginia on behalf of black soldiers and special camps of instruction were established to train them.

The book *Black Confederates* contains loads of primary documents testifying to the role of African Americans: letters, military documents, tributes, obituaries, contemporaneous newspaper articles, and more. In an 1862 letter to his uncle, a soldier at Camp Brown in Knoxville, Tennessee, wrote that his company had recently gunned down six Union soldiers and that "Jack Thomas a colored person that belongs to our company killed one of them."

An 1861 article in the *Montgomery Advertiser* says: "We are informed that Mr. G.C. Hale, of Autauga County, yesterday tendered to Governor Moore the services of a company of negroes, to assist in driving back the horde of abolition sycophants who are now talking so flippantly of reducing to a conquered province the Confederate States of the South."

The obituary of black South Carolinian Henry Brown states that he had never been a slave and had served in three wars: the Mexican, the Spanish-American, and the Civil (on the side of the South). He was given a 21-gun salute at his funeral.

In 1890, black Union veteran Joseph T. Wilson wrote in his book, *The Black Phalanx: A History of the Negro Soldiers of the United States*, that New Orleans was home to two Native Guard regiments, which comprised 3,000 "colored men." Referring to these regiments in an 1898 book, Union Captain Dan Matson said: "Here is a strange fact. We find that the Confederates themselves first armed and mustered the Negro as a solider in the late war."

Most blacks in the Confederate Army, though, were in supporting roles such as cook, musician, nurse, and the catch-all "servant." However, a lot of them ended up fighting on the battlefield, even though the South didn't officially induct black soldiers until late in the conflict. And all of them — whether inducted or not, whether solider or some other position — were eligible for military pensions from several Southern states (including Tennessee and Mississippi), and records show that many of them signed up for these benefits.

A follow-up volume, *Black Southerners in Confederate Armies*, presents even more source documents. A book from 1866 contains the recollection of a Union man whose compatriot killed a black Confederate sniper "who, through his skill as a marksman, had done more injury to our men that any dozen of his white compeers…" Union documents show Henry Marshall, a black soldier with the 14th Kentucky Cavalry, being held in Northern prisoner of war camps. A pension document from South Carolina reveals that "a free Negro who volunteered" for the army served from August 1861 to the end of the war — over three and a half years. An obituary for George Mathewson says that the former slave received "a Cross of Honor for bravery in action," based on his role as standard-bearer.

The *New York Tribune* noted "that the Rebels organized and employed 'Negro troops' a full year before our government could be persuaded to do any thing of the sort." After the Battle of Gettysburg, the *New York Herald* reported: "Among the rebel prisoners who were marched through Gettysburg there were observed seven negroes in uniform and fully accoutered as soldiers."

An article from *Smithsonian* magazine relates: "A *New York Times* correspondent with Grant in 1863 wrote: 'The guns of the rebel battery were manned almost wholly by Negroes, a single white man, or perhaps two, directing operations.'"

While it certainly couldn't be said that African Americans played a major military role in the Southern army, they were definitely there. And some of them had even volunteered. ⌗

21
ELECTRIC CARS HAVE BEEN AROUND SINCE THE 1880s

The car of the future runs completely on electricity. No more dependence on gas. No more choking the atmosphere with fumes. Whenever the possibility of electric cars is raised, the media and other commentators ooh and ahh over the potential. But this technology isn't futuristic — it's positively retro. Cars powered by electricity have been on the scene since the 1800s and actually *predate* gas-powered cars.

A blacksmith in Vermont — Thomas Davenport — built the first rotary electric motor in 1833 and used it to power a model train the next year. In the late 1830s, Scottish inventor Robert Davidson rigged a carriage with an electric motor powered by batteries. In his Pulitzer-nominated book *Taking Charge*, archaeology professor and technology historian Michael Brian Schiffer writes that this "was perhaps the first electric car."

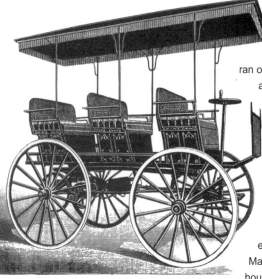

After this remarkable achievement, the idea of an electric car languished for decades. In 1881, a French experimenter debuted a personal vehicle that ran on electricity, a tricycle (ie, three wheels and a seat) for adults. In 1888, many inventors in the US, Britain, and Europe started creating three- and four-wheel vehicles — which could carry two to six people — that ran on electricity. These vehicles remained principally curiosities until May 1897, when the Pope Manufacturing Company — the country's most successful bicycle manufacturer — started selling the first commercial electric car: the Columbia Electric Phaeton, Mark III. It topped out at fifteen miles per hour, and had to be recharged every 30 miles.

Within two years, people could choose from an array of electrical carriages, buggies, wagons, trucks, bicycles, tricycles, even buses and ambulances made by numerous manufacturers.

New York City was home to a fleet of electric taxi cabs starting in 1897. The Electric Vehicle Company eventually had over 100 of them ferrying people around the Big Apple. Soon it was unleashing electric taxis in Chicago, Philadelphia, Boston, and Washington DC. By 1900, though, the company was in trouble, and seven years later it sputtered out.

As for cars powered by dead dinosaurs, Austrian engineer Siegfried Marcus attached a one-cylinder motor to a cart in 1864, driving it 500 feet and thus creating the first vehicle powered by gas (this was around 25 years after Davidson had created the first electro-car). It wasn't until 1895 that gas autos — converted carriages with a two-cylinder engine — were commercially sold (and then only in microscopic numbers).

Around the turn of the century, the average car buyer had a big choice to make: gas, electric, or steam? When the auto industry took form around 1895, nobody knew which type of vehicle was going to become the standard. During the last few years of the nineteenth century and the first few of the twentieth, over 100 companies placed their bets on electricity. According to Schiffer, "Twenty-eight percent of the 4,192 American automobiles produced in 1900 were electric. In the New York automobile show of that year more electrics were on display than gasoline or steam vehicles."

In the middle of the first decade of the 1900s, electric cars were on the decline, and their gas-eating cousins were surging ahead. With improvements in the cars and their batteries, though, electrics started a comeback in 1907, which continued through 1913. The downhill slide started the next year, and by the 1920s the market for electrics was "minuscule," to use Schiffer's word. Things never got better.

Many companies tried to combine the best of both approaches, with cars that ran on a mix of electricity and gas. The Pope Manufacturing Company, once again in the vanguard, built a working prototype in 1898. A Belgian company and a French company each brought out commercial models the next year, beating the Toyota Prius and the Honda Insight to the market by over a century. Even Ferdinand Porsche and the Mercedes Company got in on the act. Unfortunately, these hybrids never really caught on.

Didik Design — which manufactures several vehicles which run on various combinations of electricity, solar power, and human power — maintains an extensive archive on the history of electric and electro-fuel cars. According to their research, around 200 companies and individuals have manufactured electric cars. Only a few familiar names are on the list (although some of them aren't familiar as car manufacturers): Studebaker (1952-1966), General Electric (1901-1904), Braun (1977), Sears, Roebuck, and Company (1978), and Oldsmobile (1896 to the present). The vast majority have long been forgotten: Elecctra, Pfluger, Buffalo Automobile Company, Hercules, Red Bug, and Nu-Klea Starlite, to name a few. Henry Ford and Thomas Edison teamed up on an electric car, but, although some prototypes were built, it never was commercially produced. Though they have faded from mass cultural memory, electric cars have never been completely out of production.

The reasons why electrics faded into obscurity while gas cars and trucks became 99.999 percent dominant are complex and are still being debated. If only they hadn't been sidelined and had continued to develop apace, the world would be a very different place. ⌗

22
JURIES ARE ALLOWED TO JUDGE THE LAW, NOT JUST THE FACTS

In order to guard citizens against the whims of the King, the right to a trial by jury was established by the Magna Carta in 1215, and it has become one of the most sacrosanct legal aspects of British and American societies. We tend to believe that the duty of a jury is solely to determine whether someone broke the law. In fact, it's not unusual for judges to instruct juries that they are to judge only the facts in a case, while the judge will sit in judgment of the law itself. Nonsense.

Juries are the last line of defense against the power abuses of the authorities. They have the right to judge the law. Even if a defendant committed a crime, a jury can refuse to render a guilty verdict. Among the main reasons why this might happen, according to attorney Clay S. Conrad:

When the defendant has already suffered enough, when it would be unfair or against the public interest for the defendant to be convicted, when the jury disagrees with the law itself, when the prosecution or the arresting authorities have gone "too far" in the single-minded quest to arrest and convict a particular defendant, when the punishments to be imposed are excessive or when the jury suspects that the charges have been brought for political reasons or to make an unfair example of the hapless defendant...

Some of the earliest examples of jury nullification from Britain and the American Colonies were refusals to convict people who had spoken ill of the government (they were prosecuted under "seditious libel" laws) or who were practicing forbidden religions, such as Quakerism. Up to the time of the Civil War, American juries often refused to convict the brave souls who helped runaway slaves. In the 1800s, jury nullifications saved the hides of union organizers who were being prosecuted with conspiracy to restrain trade. Juries used their power to free people charged under the anti-alcohol laws of Prohibition, as well as antiwar protesters during the Vietnam era. Today, juries sometimes refuse to convict drug users (especially medical marijuana users), tax protesters, abortion protesters, gun owners, battered spouses, and people who commit "mercy killings."

Judges and prosecutors will often outright lie about the existence of this power, but centuries of court decisions and other evidence prove that jurors can vote their consciences.

When the US Constitution was created, with its Sixth Amendment guarantee of a jury trial, the most popular law dictionary of the time said that juries "may not only find things of their own knowledge, but they go according to their consciences." The first edition of Noah Webster's celebrated dictionary (1828) said that juries "decide both the law and the fact in criminal prosecutions."

Jury nullification is specifically enshrined in the constitutions of Pennsylvania, Indiana, and Maryland. The state codes of Connecticut and Illinois contain similar provisions.

The second US President, John Adams, wrote: "It is not only [the juror's] right, but his duty…to find the verdict according to his own best understanding, judgment, and conscience, though in direct opposition to the direction of the court." Similarly, Founding Father Alexander Hamilton declared: "It is essential to the security of personal rights and public liberty, that the jury should have and exercise the power to judge both of the law and of the criminal intent."

Legendary Supreme Court Chief Justice John Jay once instructed a jury:

It may not be amiss, here, Gentlemen, to remind you of the good old rule, that on questions of fact, it is the providence of the jury, on questions of law, it is the providence of the court to decide. But it must be observed that by the same law, which recognizes this reasonable distribution of jurisdiction, you have nevertheless the right to take upon yourselves to judge of both, and to determine the law as well as the fact in controversy.

The following year, 1795, Justice James Irdell declared: "[T]hough the jury will generally respect the sentiment of the court on points of law, they are not bound to deliver a verdict conformably to them." In 1817, Chief Justice John Marshall said that "the jury in a capital case were judges, as well of the law as the fact, and were bound to acquit where either was doubtful."

In more recent times, the Fourth Circuit Court of Appeals unanimously held in 1969:

If the jury feels that the law under which the defendant is accused is unjust, or that exigent circumstances justified the actions of the accused, or for any reason which appeals to their logic and passion, the jury has the power to

acquit, and the courts must abide that decision.

Three years later, the DC Circuit Court of Appeals noted: "The pages of history shine on instances of the jury's exercise of its prerogative to disregard uncontradicted evidence and instructions of the judge."

In a 1993 law journal article, federal Judge Jack B. Weinstein wrote: "When juries refuse to convict on the basis of what they think are unjust laws, they are performing their duties as jurors."

Those who try to wish away the power of jury nullification often point to cases in which racist juries have refused to convict white people charged with racial violence. As attorney Conrad shows in his book, *Jury Nullification: The Evolution of a Doctrine*, this has occurred only in very rare instances. Besides, it's ridiculous to try to stamp out or deny a certain power just because it can be used for bad ends as well as good. What form of power hasn't been misused at least once in a while?

The Fully Informed Jury Association (FIJA) is the best-known organization seeking to tell all citizens about their powers as jurors. People have been arrested for simply handing out FIJA literature in front of courthouses. During jury selections, FIJA members have been excluded solely on the grounds that they belong to the group.

FIJA also seeks laws that would require judges to tell jurors that they can and should judge the law, but this has been an uphill battle, to say the least. In a still-standing decision (*Sparf and Hansen v. US*, 1895), the Supreme Court ruled that judges don't have to let jurors know their full powers. In cases where the defense has brought up jury nullification during the proceedings, judges have sometimes held the defense attorney in contempt. Still, 21 state legislatures have introduced informed-jury legislation, with three of them passing it through one chamber (ie, House or Senate).

Quite obviously, the justice system is terrified of this power, which is all the more reason for us to know about it. ▢

23
THE POLICE AREN'T LEGALLY OBLIGATED TO PROTECT YOU

Without even thinking about it, we take it as a given that the police must protect each of us. That's their whole reason for existence, right?

While this might be true in a few jurisdictions in the US and Canada, it is actually the exception, not the rule. In general, court decisions and state laws have held that cops don't have to do a damn thing to help you when you're in danger.

In the only book devoted exclusively to the subject, *Dial 911 and Die*, attorney Richard W. Stevens writes:

It was the most shocking thing I learned in law school. I was studying Torts in my

first year at the University of San Diego School of Law, when I came upon the case of *Hartzler v. City of San Jose*. In that case I discovered the secret truth: *the government owes no duty to protect individual citizens from criminal attack.* Not only did the California courts hold to that rule, the California legislature had enacted a statute to make sure the courts couldn't change the rule.

But this doesn't apply to just the wild, upside down world of Kalifornia. Stevens cites laws and cases for every state — plus Washington DC, Puerto Rico, the Virgin Islands, and Canada — which reveal the same thing. If the police fail to protect you, even through sheer incompetence and negligence, don't expect that you or your next of kin will be able to sue.

Even in the nation's heartland, in bucolic Iowa, you can't depend on 911. In 1987, two men broke into a family's home, tied up the parents, slit the mother's throat, raped the 16-year-old daughter, and drove off with the 12-year old daughter (whom they later murdered). The emergency dispatcher couldn't be bothered with immediately sending police to chase the kidnappers/murders/rapists while the abducted little girl was still alive. First he had to take calls about a parking violation downtown and a complaint about harassing phone calls. When he got around to the kidnapping, he didn't issue an all-points bulletin but instead told just one officer to come back to the police station, not even mentioning that it was an emergency. Even more blazing negligence ensued, but suffice it to say that when the remnants of the family sued the city and the police, their case was summarily dismissed before going to trial. The state appeals court upheld the decision, claiming that the authorities have no duty to protect individuals.

Similarly, people in various states have been unable to successfully sue over the following situations:

- ☠ **when 911 systems have been shut down for maintenance**

- ☠ **when a known stalker kills someone**

- ☠ **when the police pull over but don't arrest a drunk driver who runs over someone later that night**

- ☠ **when a cop known to be violently unstable shoots a driver he pulled over for an inadequate muffler**

- ☠ **when authorities know in advance of a plan to commit murder but do nothing to stop it**

- ☠ **when parole boards free violent psychotics, including child rapist-murderers**

- ☠ **when felons escape from prison and kill someone**

- ☠ **when houses burn down because the fire department didn't respond promptly**

- ☠ **when children are beaten to death in foster homes**

A minority of states do offer a tiny bit of hope. In eighteen states, citizens have successfully sued over failure to protect, but even here the grounds have been very narrow. Usually, the police and the victim must have had a prior "special relationship" (for example, the authorities must have promised protection to this specific individual in the past). And, not surprisingly, many of these states have issued contradictory court rulings, or a conflict exists between state law and the rulings of the courts.

Don't look to Constitution for help. "In its landmark decision of *DeShaney v. Winnebago County Department of Social Services*," Stevens writes, "the US Supreme Court declared that the Constitution does not impose a duty on the state and local governments to protect the citizens from criminal harm."

All in all, as Stevens says, you'd be much better off owning a gun and learning how to use it. Even in those cases where you could successfully sue, this victory comes only after years (sometimes more than a decade) of wrestling with the justice system and only after you've been gravely injured or your loved one has been snuffed. ⌗

24
THE GOVERNMENT CAN TAKE YOUR HOUSE AND LAND, THEN SELL THEM TO PRIVATE CORPORATIONS

It's not an issue that gets much attention, but the government has the right to seize your house, business, and/or land, forcing you into the street. This mighty power, called "eminent domain," is enshrined in the US Constitution's Fifth Amendment: "...nor shall private property be taken for public use without just compensation." Every single state constitution also stipulates that a person whose property is taken must be justly compensated and that the property must be put to public use. This should mean that if your house is smack-dab in the middle of a proposed highway, the government can take it, pay you market value, and build the highway.

Whether or not this is a power the government should have is very much open to question, but what makes it worse is the abuse of this supposedly limited power. Across the country, local governments are stealing their citizens' property, then turning around and selling it to corporations for the construction of malls, condominiums, parking lots, racetracks, office complexes, factories, etc.

The Institute for Justice — the country's only nonprofit, public-interest law firm with a libertarian philosophy — spends a good deal of time protecting individuals and small businesses from greedy corporations and their partners in crime: bureaucrats armed with eminent domain. In 2003, it released a report on the use of "governmental condemnation" (another name for eminent domain) for private gain. No central data collection for this trend exists, and only one state (Connecticut) keeps statistics on it. Using court records, media accounts, and information from involved parties, the Institute found over *10,000* such abuses in 41 states from 1998 through 2002. Of these, the legal process had been initiated against 3,722 properties, and condemnation had been threatened against 6,560 properties. (Remember, this is condemnation solely for the benefit of private parties, not for so-called legitimate reasons of "public use.")

In one instance, the city of Hurst, Texas, condemned 127 homes so that a mall could expand. Most of the families moved under the pressure, but ten chose to stay and fight. The Institute writes:

A Texas trial judge refused to stay the condemnations while the suit was ongoing, so the residents lost their homes. Leonard Prohs had to move while his wife was in the hospital with brain cancer. She died only five days after their house was demolished. Phyllis Duval's husband also was in the hospital with cancer at the time they were required to move. He died one month after the demolition. Of the ten couples, three spouses died and four others suffered heart attacks during the dispute and litigation. In court, the owners presented evidence that the land surveyor who designed the roads for the mall had been told to change the path of one road to run through eight of the houses of the owners challenging the condemnations.

In another case, wanting to "redevelop" Main Street, the city of East Hartford, Connecticut, used eminent domain to threaten a bakery/deli that had been in that spot for 93 years, owned and operated by the same family during that whole time. Thus coerced, the family sold the business for $1.75 million, and the local landmark was destroyed. But the redevelopment fell through, so the lot now stands empty and the city is in debt.

The city of Cypress, California, wanted Costco to build a retail store on an 18-acre plot of land. Trouble was, the Cottonwood Christian Center already owned the land fair and square, and was planning to build a church on it. The city council used eminent domain to seize the land, saying that the new church would be a "public nuisance" and would "blight" the area (which is right beside a horse-racing track). The Christian Center got a federal injunction to stop the condemnation, and the city appealed this decision. To avoid further protracted legal nightmares, the church group consented to trade its land for another tract in the vicinity.

But all of this is small potatoes compared to what's going on in Riviera Beach, Florida:

City Council members voted unanimously to approve a $1.25 billion redevelopment plan with the authority to use eminent domain to condemn at least 1,700 houses and apartments and dislocate 5,100 people. The city will then take the property and sell the land to commercial yachting, shipping, and tourism companies.

If approved by the state, it will be one of the biggest eminent domain seizures in US history.

In 1795, the Supreme Court referred to eminent domain as "the despotic power." Over two centuries later, they continue to be proven right. ♂

25
THE SUPREME COURT HAS RULED THAT YOU'RE ALLOWED TO INGEST ANY DRUG, ESPECIALLY IF YOU'RE AN ADDICT

In the early 1920s, Dr. Linder was convicted of selling one morphine tablet and three cocaine tablets to a patient who was addicted to narcotics. The Supreme Court overturned the conviction, declaring that providing an addicted patient with a fairly small amount of drugs is an acceptable medical practice "when designed temporarily to alleviate an addict's pains." (*Linder v. United States*.)

In 1962, the Court heard the case of a man who had been sent to the clink under a California state law that made being an addict a criminal offense. Once again, the verdict was tossed out, with the Supremes saying that punishing an addict for being an addict is cruel and unusual and, thus, unconstitutional. (*Robinson v. California*.)

Six years later, the Supreme Court reaffirmed these principles in *Powell v. Texas*. A man who was arrested for being drunk in public said that, because he was an alcoholic, he couldn't help it. He invoked the *Robinson* decision as precedent. The Court upheld his conviction because it had been based on an action (being wasted in public), not on the general condition of his addiction to booze. Justice White supported this decision, yet for different reasons than the others. In his concurring opinion, he expanded *Robinson*:

If it cannot be a crime to have an irresistible compulsion to use narcotics,... I do

not see how it can constitutionally be a crime to yield to such a compulsion. **Punishing an addict for using drugs convicts for addiction under a different name. Distinguishing between the two crimes is like forbidding criminal conviction for being sick with flu or epilepsy, but permitting punishment for running a fever or having a convulsion. Unless** *Robinson* **is to be abandoned, the use of narcotics by an addict must be beyond the reach of the criminal law. Similarly, the chronic alcoholic with an irresistible urge to consume alcohol should not be punishable for drinking or for being drunk.**

Commenting on these cases, Superior Court Judge James P. Gray, an outspoken critic of drug prohibition, has recently written:

What difference is there between alcohol and any other dangerous and sometimes addictive drug? The primary difference is that one is legal while the others are not. And the US Supreme Court has said as much on at least two occasions, finding both in 1925 and 1962 that to punish a person for the disease of drug addiction violated the Constitution's prohibition on cruel and unusual punishment. If that is true, why do we continue to prosecute addicted people for taking these drugs, when it would be unconstitutional to prosecute them for their addiction?

Judge Gray gets right to the heart of the matter: "In effect, this 'forgotten precedent' says that one can only be constitutionally punishable for one's *conduct*, such as assaults, burglary, and driving under the influence, and not simply for what one puts into one's own body."

If only the Supreme Court and the rest of the justice/law-enforcement complex would apply these decisions, we'd be living in a saner society. ▯

26
THE AGE OF CONSENT IN MOST OF THE US IS NOT EIGHTEEN

The accepted wisdom tells us that the age at which a person can legally consent to sex in the US is eighteen. Before this line of demarcation, a person is "jailbait" or "chicken." On their eighteenth birthday, they become "legal." But in the majority of states, this isn't the case.

It's up to each state to determine its own age of consent. Only fifteen states have put theirs at eighteen, with the rest going lower. Eight have set the magic point at the seventeenth birthday. The most popular age is sixteen, with 27 states and Washington DC setting the ability to sexually consent there. (Hawaii's age of consent had been fourteen until mid-2001, when it was bumped to sixteen.)

Of course, as with anything regarding the law, there are considerable shades of gray. For one thing, these laws don't apply if the lovers are married. The age of consent for marriage, especially with parental permission, is usually lower than the age of sexual consent.

The Constitution of the State of South Carolina says that females aged fourteen and up can consent to sex, but state law appears to set the age at sixteen.

In a lot of states, the age of the older partner is a consideration. For example, Tennessee doesn't consider sex with someone aged thirteen to seventeen to be statutory rape if the elder partner is less than four years older. So a nineteen-year-old could get it on with a sixteen-year-old without breaking the law. The most extreme example of this rule is in Delaware. If you're 30 or older, boffing a sixteen- or seventeen-year-old is a felony. But if you're 29 or younger, it's perfectly legal.

And let's not even get into Georgia's Public Law 16-6-18, which outlaws sex between anyone who isn't married, no matter what their ages or genders.

Then, of course, we have the laws regarding same-sex relations, which are completely illegal in fifteen or so states. In almost all of the others states, the age of consent for gay sex is the same as that for het-sex. Two exceptions are Nevada and New Hampshire, which both allow sixteen-year-olds to consent to a member of the opposite sex, but set the limit at eighteen for those who go the other way. Somewhat startlingly, even though New Mexico's age of consent for straights is seventeen, it's thirteen for gays and lesbians.

The situation around the world varies even more than within the US. The age of consent in the UK is sixteen, except in Northern Ireland, where it's a year older. Various territories in Australia set the age at sixteen or seventeen, and in Canada it's universally fourteen. The lowest age — in a few countries, such as Chile and Mexico — is twelve. Only one country is known to have set the age above eighteen — Tunisia, which feels that twenty is the acceptable age. 🖵

27
MOST SCIENTISTS DON'T READ
ALL OF THE ARTICLES THEY CITE

Every scientific discovery builds on what came before. Because of this, research papers are chock-full of references to previous papers, leading you to believe that those older studies actually have been read and digested and are now being expanded upon.

After noticing that a lot of citations with identical mistakes were showing up in various papers, two researchers at the University of California, Los Angeles, set out to study the problem. They looked at the way well-known, heavily-cited papers had been referenced in subsequent papers. Regarding an influential paper on crystals published in 1973, *New Scientist* explains:

They found it had been cited in other papers 4300 times, with 196 citations containing misprints in the volume, page or year. But despite the fact that a billion different versions of erroneous reference are possible, they counted only 45. The most popular mistake appeared 78 times.

Obviously, these pursuers of scientific truths hadn't actually read the original paper, but had just clipped the reference from another paper, a trick they probably learned in college and never stopped using. Of course, some of the scientists who got the citation right hadn't read the paper, either. In the final analysis:

The model shows that the distribution of misprinted citations of the 1973 paper

could only have arisen if 78 percent of all the citations, including the correct ones, were "cut and pasted" from a secondary source. Many of those who got it right were simply lucky. 🗇

28
LOUIS PASTEUR SUPPRESSED EXPERIMENTS THAT DIDN'T SUPPORT HIS THEORIES

One of the greatest scientific duels in history occurred between those who believed that micro-organisms spontaneously generate in decaying organic matter and those who believed that the tiny creatures migrated there from the open air. From the late 1850s to the late 1870s, the eminent French chemist and microbiologist Louis Pasteur was locked in a death-match with proponents of spontaneous generation, especially Felix Pouchet.

The two camps performed experiments one after the other, both to prove their pet theory and to disprove the opponent's. As we know, Pasteur won the debate: The fact that microbes travel through the air is now accepted as a given, with spontaneous generation relegated to the slag-heap of quaint, discarded scientific ideas. But Pasteur didn't win fair and square.

It turns out that some of Pasteur's experiments gave strong *support* to the notion that rotting organic matter produces life. Of course, years later those experiments were realized to have been flawed, but at the time they buttressed the position of Pasteur's enemies. So he kept them secret.

In his myth-busting book *Einstein's Luck*, medical and scientific historian John Waller writes: "In fact, throughout his feud with Pouchet, Pasteur described in his notebooks as 'successful' any experiment that seemed to disprove spontaneous generation and 'unsuccessful' any that violated his own private beliefs and experimental expectations."

When Pasteur's rivals performed experiments that supported their theory, Pasteur would not publicly replicate those studies. In one case, he simply refused to perform the experiment or even discuss it. In another, he hemmed and hawed so long that his rival gave up in exasperation. Waller notes: "Revealingly, although Pasteur publicly ascribed Bastian's results to sloppy methodology, in private he and his team took them rather more seriously. As Gerald Geison's study of Pasteur's notebooks has recently revealed, Pasteur's team spent several weeks secretly testing Bastian's findings and refining their own ideas on the distribution of germs in the environment."

Pasteur would rail at his rivals and even his mentor when he thought they weren't scrupulously following the scientific method, yet he had no qualms about trashing it when doing so suited his aims. Luckily for him, he was on the right side of the debate. And just why was he so cocksure that spontaneous generation was wrong? It had nothing to do with science. "In his notes he repeatedly insisted that only the Creator-God had ever exercised the power to convert the inanimate into the living," writes Waller. "The possibility that life could be created anew without man first discovering the secrets of the Creator was rejected without any attempt at scientific justification."

29
THE CREATOR OF THE GAIA HYPOTHESIS SUPPORTS NUCLEAR POWER

James Lovelock is one of the icons of the environmental movement. His idea that the Earth is a self-regulating, living organism (the GAIA hypothesis, first expounded in his 1979 book *GAIA: A New Look at Life on Earth*) provides the philosophical underpinning of environmentalism.

So it may be surprising that Lovelock is an enthusiastic supporter of nuclear energy, which he says has "great benefits and small risks." In the preface to the seemingly paradoxical book *Environmentalists for Nuclear Energy*, he writes: "I want to put it to you that the dangers of continuing to burn fossil fuels (oil, gas, coal) as our main energy source are far greater and they threaten not just individuals but civilization itself." The answer, he maintains, is the clean energy from nuke plants, which produce almost nothing that clogs up the atmosphere. As for what to do with all that radioactive waste, Lovelock has a shocking answer:

Natural ecosystems can stand levels of continuous radiation that would be intolerable in a city. The land around the failed Chernobyl power station was evacuated because its high radiation intensity made it unsafe for people, but this radioactive land is now rich in wildlife, much more so than neighboring populated areas. We call the ash from nuclear power nuclear waste and worry about its safe disposal. I wonder if instead we should use it as an incorruptible guardian of the beautiful places of the Earth. Who would dare cut down a forest in which was the storage place of nuclear ash?

Lovelock does admit that nuclear power is "potentially harmful to people," something that his brethren in the group Environmentalists for Nuclear Power often try to downplay. Truthfully, some of their points are good ones. More people have been killed by coal-mining than by nuclear power, even when you factor in the shorter time that nuclear power has existed. Most of the radiation we get zapped with comes from outer space (around two-thirds) and medical procedures (around a third), with only a smidgen from nuke plants.

Still, when you know about all the unpublicized accidents and near-meltdowns that have occurred, it's hard to be quite so blasé about the dangers. After all, the group's own literature says, "Nuclear energy is a very clean energy if it is well designed, well-built, well operated, and well managed." Trouble is, it's often none of those things. Design flaws, human error, corruption, incompetence, greed, and toothless oversight mean that in the real world, nuke plants often don't work as advertised. ⊡

30
GENETICALLY-ENGINEERED HUMANS HAVE ALREADY BEEN BORN

The earthshaking news appeared in the medical journal *Human Reproduction* under the impenetrable headline: "Mitochondria in Human Offspring Derived From Ooplasmic Transplantation." The media put the story in heavy rotation for one day, then forgot about it. We all forgot about it.

But the fact remains that the world is now populated by dozens of children who were genetically engineered. It still sounds like science fiction, yet it's true.

In the first known application of germline gene therapy — in which an individual's genes are changed in a way that can be passed to offspring — doctors at a reproductive facility in New Jersey announced in March 2001 that nearly 30 healthy babies had been born with DNA from *three* people: dad, mom, and a second woman. Fifteen were the product of the fertility clinic, with the other fifteen or so coming from elsewhere.

The doctors believe that one cause for failure of women to conceive is that their ova contain old mitochondria (if you don't remember your high school biology class, mitochondria are the part of cells that provides energy). These sluggish eggs fail to attach to the uterine wall when fertilized. In order to soup them up, scientists injected them with mitochondria from a younger woman. Since mitochondria contain DNA, the kids have the genetic material of all three parties. The DNA from the "other woman" can even be passed down along the female line.

The big problem is that no one knows what effects this will have on the children or their progeny. In fact, this substitution of mitochondria hasn't been studied extensively on animals, never mind *homo sapiens*. The doctors reported that the kids are healthy, but they neglected to mention something crucial. Although the fertility clinic's technique resulted in fifteen babies, a total of seventeen fetuses had been created. One of them had been aborted, and the other miscarried. Why? Both of them had a rare genetic disorder, Turner syndrome, which only strikes females. Ordinarily, just one in 2,500 females is born with this condition, in which one of the X chromosomes is incomplete or totally missing. Yet two out of these seventeen fetuses had developed it.

If we assume that nine of the fetuses were female (around 50 percent), then two of the nine female fetuses had this rare condition. Internal documents from the fertility clinic admit that this amazingly high rate might be due to the ooplasmic transfer.

Even before the revelation about Turner syndrome became known, many experts were appalled that the technique had been used. A responding article in *Human Reproduction* said, in a dry understatement: "Neither the safety nor efficacy of this method has been adequately investigated." Ruth Deech, chair of Britain's Human Fertilization and Embryology Authority, told the BBC: "There is a risk, not just to the baby, but to future generations which we really can't assess at the moment."

The number of children who have been born as a result of this technique is unknown. The original article gave the number as "nearly thirty," but this was in early 2001. At that time, at least two of the mutant children were already one year old.

Dr. Joseph Cummin, professor emeritus of biology at the University of Western Ontario, says that no further information about these 30 children has appeared in the medical literature or the media. As far as additional children born with two mommies and a daddy, Cummin says that a report out of Norway in 2003 indicated that ooplasmic transfer has been used to correct mitochondrial disease. He opines: "It seems likely that the transplants are going on, but very, very quietly in a regulatory vacuum, perhaps." ⛝

31
THE INSURANCE INDUSTRY WANTS TO GENETICALLY TEST ALL POLICY HOLDERS

The insurance industry's party line is that it doesn't want to genetically test people who sign up for policies, a practice that would detect a predisposition to develop cancer, multiple sclerosis, and other diseases and disorders. The industry's internal documents tell a completely different story, though.

While researching *War Against the Weak* — his sweeping history of eugenics (and its successor, genetics) in the United States and Germany — Edwin Black found two reports written by insurers for insurers. "Genetic Information and Medical Expense" — published in June 2000 by the American Academy of Actuaries — intones that an inability to ask for genetic tests "would have a direct impact on premium rates, ultimately raising the cost of insurance for everyone."

A paper issued by the same group in spring 2002 goes further, envisioning a nightmare scenario in which the entire insurance industry collapses. The genetically impure can't be weeded out, thus meaning that more of them get covered. Because of this, the insurers have to pay out more benefits, which drives up premiums for everybody. This causes some people with perfect chromosomes to be unable to afford insurance, which means a higher percentage of the insured are chromosomally challenged. A downward spiral has started, with more benefits paid out, higher premiums charged, fewer healthy people covered, more benefits, higher premiums, fewer healthy people, etc. This, the report warns, "could eventually cause the insurers to become insolvent."

In the UK, insurance companies were widely screening applicants for genetic red flags until Parliament slapped a moratorium on the practice in 2001, allowing only one type of test to be used. British companies argue that they will go belly-up if the ban isn't lifted soon. Based on this alone, it's ridiculous for the US insurance industry to claim it isn't hoping to use these tests.

With the fate of the insurance racket supposedly hanging in the balance, how long can it be before genetic screening is mandatory when applying for health or life coverage? ⛢

32
SMOKING CAUSES PROBLEMS OTHER THAN LUNG CANCER AND HEART DISEASE

The fact that smoking causes lung disease and oral cancer isn't exactly news, and only tobacco industry executives would express (feigned) shock at being told. But cigarettes can lead to a whole slew of problems involving every system of your tar-filled body, and most people aren't aware of this.

The American Council on Science and Health's book *Cigarettes: What the Warning Label Doesn't Tell You* is the first comprehensive look at the medical evidence of all types of harm triggered by smoking. Referencing over 450 articles from medical journals and reviewed by

45 experts — mainly medical doctors and PhDs — if this book doesn't convince you to quit, nothing will.

Among some of the things that cancer sticks do:

☠ Besides cancers of the head, neck, and lungs, ciggies are especially connected to cancers of the bladder, kidney, pancreas, and cervix. Newer evidence is adding leukemia and colorectal cancer to the list. Recent studies have also found at least a doubling of risk among smokers for cancers of the vulva and penis, as well as an eight-fold risk of anal cancer for men and a nine-fold risk for women.

☠ Smoking trashes the ability of blood to flow, which results in a sixteen-fold greater risk of peripheral vascular disease. This triggers pain in the legs and arms, which often leads to an inability to walk and, in some instances, gangrene and/or amputation. Seventy-six percent of all cases are caused by smoking, more than for any other factor, including diabetes, obesity, and high blood pressure.

☠ Smokers are at least two to three times more likely to develop the heartbreak of psoriasis. Even if that doesn't happen, they'll look old before their time. The American Council tells us, "Smokers in their 40s have facial wrinkles similar to those of nonsmokers in their 60s."

☠ Smokers require more anesthesia for surgery, and they recover much more slowly. In fact, wounds of all kinds take longer to heal for smokers.

☠ Puffing helps to weaken bones, soft tissue, and spinal discs, causing all kinds of musculo-skeletal pain, more broken bones and ruptured discs, and longer healing time. "A non-smoker's leg heals an average of 80 percent faster than a smoker's broken leg."

☠ Smoking is heavily related to osteoporosis, the loss of bone mass, which results in brittle bones and more breaks.

☠ Cigarettes interfere with your ability to have kids. "The fertility rates of women who smoke are about 30 percent lower than those of nonsmokers." If you're an idiot who continues to smoke while you're expecting — even in this day and age, some people, including stars Catherine Zeta-Jones and Courtney Love, do this — you increase the risks of miscarriage, stillbirth, premature birth, low birth weight, underdevelopment, and cleft pallet. If your child is able to survive outside the womb, it will have a heavily elevated risk of crib death (SIDS), allergies, and intellectual impairment.

☠ Smoking also does a serious number on sperm, resulting in more deformed cells, less ability of them to swim, smaller loads, and a drastic decrease in overall number of the little fellas. The larger population of misshapen sperm probably increases the risk of miscarriages and birth defects, so even if mommy doesn't smoke, daddy could still cause problems. What's more, because smoking hurts blood flow, male smokers are at least twice as likely to be unable to get it up.

☠ Besides shutting down blood flow to the little head, smoking interferes with the blood going to the big head in both sexes. This causes one quarter of all strokes. It also makes these strokes more likely to occur earlier in life and more likely to be fatal.

☠ "Depression — whether viewed as a trait, a symptom or a diagnosable disorder — is over-represented among smokers." Unfortunately, it's unclear how the two are related. Does smoking cause depression, or does depression lead to smoking? Or, most likely, do the two feed on each other in a vicious cycle?

☠ "Smokers experience sudden hearing loss an average of 16 years earlier than do never smokers."

☠ Smokers and former smokers have an increased risk of developing cataracts, abnormal eye movements, inflammation of the optic nerve, permanent blindness from lack of blood flow, and the most severe form of macular degeneration.

☠ Lighting up increases plaque, gum disease, and tooth loss.

☠ It also makes it likelier that you'll develop diabetes, stomach ulcers, colon polyps, and Crohn's disease.

☠ Smoking trashes the immune system in myriad ways, with the overall result being that you're more susceptible to disease and allergies.

☠ And let's not forget that second-hand smoke has horrible effects on the estimated 42 percent of toddlers and infants who are forced to inhale it in their homes:

According to the Environmental Protection Agency (EPA), children's "passive smoking," as it is called, results in hundreds of thousands of cases of bronchitis, pneumonia, ear infections, and worsened asthma. Worse yet, the Centers for Disease Control and Prevention estimates that 702 children younger than one year die each year as a result of sudden infant death syndrome (SIDS), worsened asthma and serious respiratory infections.

It's very surprising to note that smoking can have a few health *benefits*. Because they zap women's estrogen levels, cigarettes can lead to less endometriosis and other conditions related to the hormone. Smoking also decreases the risk of developing osteoarthritis in the knees, perhaps because the pliability of thin bones takes some pressure off of the cartilage. And because it jacks up dopamine levels, it helps ward off Parkinson's disease. Of course, these benefits seem to be side effects of the hazards of smoking, so the trade-off hardly seems worth it. ロ

33
HERDS OF MILK-PRODUCING COWS ARE RIFE WITH BOVINE LEUKEMIA VIRUS

Bovine leukemia virus is a cancer-causing microbe in cattle. Just how many cows have it? The US Department of Agriculture reports that nationwide, *89 percent* of herds contain cows with BLV. The most infected region is the Southeast, where 99 percent of herds have the tumor-causing bug. In some herds across the country, almost every single animal is infected. A 1980 study across Canada uncovered a lower but none-too-reassuring rate of 40 percent.

BLV is transmitted through milk. Since the milk from all cows in a herd is mixed before processing, if even a single cow is infected, all milk from that herd will have BLV swimming in it. Citing an article in *Science*, oncologist Robert Kradjian, MD, warns that 90 to 95 percent of milk starts out tainted. Of course, pasteurization — when done the right way — kills BLV, but the process isn't perfect. And if you drink raw milk, odds are you're gulping down bovine leukemia virus.

Between dairy cows and their cousins that are used for meat (who tend to be infected at lower rates), it appears that a whole lot of BLV is getting inside us. A 2001 study in *Breast Cancer Research* detected antibodies to the bovine leukemia virus in blood samples from 77 out of 100 volunteers. Furthermore, BLV showed up more often in breast tissue from women with breast cancer than in the tissue from healthy women. Several medical studies have found positive correlations between higher intake of milk/beef and increased incidence of leukemia or lymphoma in humans, although other studies haven't found a correlation.

No hard evidence has yet linked BLV to diseases in humans, but do you feel comfortable knowing that cow cancer cells are in your body? 🖰

34
MOST DOCTORS DON'T KNOW THE RADIATION LEVEL OF CAT SCANS

Using extended doses of encircling X-rays, CAT scans give a detailed look inside your body, revealing not only bones but soft tissue and blood vessels, as well. According to the health site Imaginis.com, over 70,000 places around the world offer CAT scans to detect and diagnose tumors, heart disease, osteoporosis, blood clots, spinal fractures, nerve damage, and lots of other problems. Because it can uncover so much, its use has become widespread and continues to rise. In fact, healthy people are getting scans just to see if anything might be wrong, kind of like a routine check-up.

The downside, and it's a doozy, is that a CAT scan jolts you with *100 to 250 times* the dose of radiation that you get from a chest X-ray. What's even more alarming is that most doctors apparently don't know this.

An emergency physician from the Yale School of Medicine surveyed 45 of his colleagues about the pros and cons of CAT scans. A mere nine of them said that they tell patients about the radiation. This might be just as well, in a weird way, since most of them had absolutely no clue about how much radiation CAT scans give off. When asked to compare the blast from a chest X-ray to the blast from a CAT scan, only 22 percent of the docs got it right. As for the other three-quarters, *The Medical Post* relates:

Three of the doctors said the dose was either less than or equal to a chest X-ray.

Twenty (44%) of the doctors said the dose was greater than a chest X-ray, but less than 10 times the dose. Just over one-fifth of the doctors (22%) said the radiation dose from a CT was more than 10 times that of an X-ray but less than 100 times the dose.

Only ten of them knew that a single CAT scan equals 100 to 250 chest X-rays, while two thought that the scans were even worse than that.

Feel free to give your doc a pop quiz during your next office visit. ⏚

35
MEDICATION ERRORS KILL THOUSANDS EACH YEAR

Next time you get a prescription filled, look at the label very carefully. Getting the wrong drug or the wrong dosage kills hundreds or thousands of people each year, with many times that number getting injured.

Renegade health reporter Nicholas Regush — a self-imposed exile from ABC News — provides a long list of specific problems:

Poor handwriting. Verbal orders. Ambiguous orders. Prescribing errors. Failure to write orders. Unapproved uses. When the order is not modified or cancelled. Look-alike and sound-alike drug names. Dangerous abbreviations. Faulty drug

distribution systems in hospital. Failure to read the label or poor labeling. Lack of knowledge about drugs. Lack of knowledge concerning proper dose. Lack of knowledge concerning route of administration. Ad nauseam.

After pouring over death certificates, sociology professor David Philips — an expert in mortality statistics — determined that drug errors kill 7,000 people each year in the US. His study was published in *The Lancet*, probably the most prestigious medical journal in the world. The Institute of Medicine, a branch of the National Academies of Science, also estimated 7,000. Interestingly, the Food and Drug Administration published the lowball figure of 365 annually (one per day). But even the FDA admits that such bungling injures *1.3 million* people each year.

New York *Newsday* cited several specific cases, such as: "In 1995, a Texas doctor wrote an illegible prescription causing the patient to receive not only the wrong medication, but at eight times the drug's usually recommended strength. The patient, Ramon Vasquez, died. In 1999, a court ordered the doctor and pharmacy to pay the patient's family a total of $450,000, the largest amount ever awarded in an illegible prescription case."

Besides doctors' indecipherable chicken scratch, similar-sounding drug names are another big culprit. Pharmaceutical companies have even started warning medical professionals to be careful with the cookie-cutter names of their products. In a typical example, Celebrex, Cerebyx, Celexa, and Zyprexa sometimes get confused. (Respectively, they're used to treat arthritis, seizures, depression, and psychosis.) According to WebMD: "Bruce Lambert, an assistant professor of pharmacy administration at the University of Illinois at Chicago, says there are 100,000 potential pairings of drug names that could be confused." ▢

36
PRESCRIPTION DRUGS KILL OVER 100,000 ANNUALLY

Even higher than the number of people who die from medication errors is the number of people who die from medication, period. Even when a prescription drug is dispensed properly, there's no guarantee it won't end up killing you.

A remarkable study in the *Journal of the American Medical Association* revealed that prescription drugs kill around 106,000 people in the US every year, which ranks prescription drugs as the fourth leading cause of death. Furthermore, each years sees 2,216,000 *serious* adverse drug reactions (defined as "those that required hospitalization, were permanently disabling, or resulted in death").

The authors of this 1998 study performed a meta-analysis on 39 previous studies covering 32 years. They factored out such things as medication errors, abuse of prescription drugs, and adverse reactions not considered serious. Plus, the study involved only people who had either been hospitalized due to drug reactions or who experienced reactions while in the hospital. People who died immediately (and, thus, never went to the hospital) and those whose deaths weren't realized to be due to prescription drugs were not included, so the true figure is probably higher.

Four years later, another study in the *JAMA* warned:

Patient exposure to new drugs with unknown toxic effects may be extensive. Nearly 20 million patients in the United States took at least 1 of the 5 drugs withdrawn from the market between September 1997 and September 1998. Three of these 5 drugs were new, having been on the market for less than 2 years. Seven drugs approved since 1993 and subsequently withdrawn from the market have been reported as possibly contributing to 1002 deaths.

Examining warnings added to drug labels through the years, the study's authors found that of the new chemical entities approved from 1975 to 1999, 10 percent "acquired a new black box warning or were withdrawn from the market" by 2000. Using some kind of high-falutin' statistical process, they estimate that the "probability of a new drug acquiring black box warnings or being withdrawn from the market over 25 years was 20%."

A statement released by one of the study's coauthors — Sidney Wolfe, MD, Director of Public Citizen's Health Studies Group — warned:

In 1997, 39 new drugs were approved by the FDA. As of now [May 2002], five of them (Rezulin, Posicor, Duract, Raxar and Baycol) have been taken off the market and an additional two (Trovan, an antibiotic and Orgaran, an anticoagulant) have had new box warnings. Thus, seven drugs approved that year (18% of the 39 drugs approved) have already been withdrawn or had a black box warning in just four years after approval. Based on our study, 20% of drugs will be withdrawn or have a

black box warning within 25 years of coming on the market. The drugs approved in 1997 have already almost "achieved" this in only four years — with 21 years to go.

How does this happen? Before the FDA approves a new drug, it must undergo clinical trials. These trials aren't performed by the FDA, though — they're done by the drug companies themselves. These trials often use relatively few patients, and they usually select patients most likely to react well to the drug. On top of that, the trials are often for a short period of time (weeks), even though real-world users may be on a drug for months or years at a time. Dr. Wolfe points out that even when adverse effects show up during clinical trials, the drugs are sometimes released anyway, and they end up being taken off the market because of those same adverse effects.

Postmarketing reporting of adverse effects isn't much better. The FDA runs a program to collect reports of problems with drugs, but compliance is voluntary. The generally accepted estimate in the medical community is that a scant 10 percent of individual instances of adverse effects are reported to the FDA, which would mean that the problem is ten times worse than we currently believe.

Drugs aren't released when they've been proven safe; they're released when enough FDA bureaucrats — many of whom have worked for the pharmaceutical companies or will work for them in the future — can be convinced that it's kinda safe. Basically, the use of prescription drugs by the general public can be seen as widespread, long-term clinical trials to determine their *true* safety.

We are all guinea pigs. ☐

37
WORK KILLS MORE PEOPLE THAN WAR

The United Nations' International Labor Organization has revealed some horrifying stats:

The ILO estimates that approximately two million workers lose their lives annually due to occupational injuries and illnesses, with accidents causing at least 350,000 deaths a year. For every fatal accident, there are an estimated 1,000 non-fatal injuries, many of which result in lost earnings, permanent disability and poverty. The death toll at work, much of which is attributable to unsafe working practices, is the equivalent of 5,000 workers dying each day, three persons every minute.

This is more than double the figure for deaths from warfare (650,000 deaths per year). According to the ILO's SafeWork programme, work kills more people than alcohol and drugs together and the resulting loss in Gross Domestic Product is 20 times greater than all official development assistance to the developing countries.

Each year, 6,570 US workers die because of injuries at work, while 60,225 meet their maker due to occupational diseases. (Meanwhile, 13.2 million get hurt, and 1.1 million develop illnesses that don't kill them.) On an average day, two or three workers are fatally shot, two fall to their deaths, one is killed after being smashed by a vehicle, and one is electrocuted. Each year, around 30 workers die of heat stroke, and another 30 expire from carbon monoxide.

Although blue collar workers face a lot of the most obvious dangers, those slaving in offices or stores must contend with toxic air, workplace violence, driving accidents, and (especially for the health-care workers) transmissible diseases. The Occupational Safety and Health Administration warns that poisonous indoor air in nonindustrial workplaces causes "[t]housands of heart disease deaths [and] hundreds of lung cancer deaths" each year.

But hey, everybody has to go sometime, right? And since we spend so much of our lives in the workplace, it's only logical that a lot of deaths happen — or at least are set into motion — on the job. This explanation certainly is true to an extent, but it doesn't excuse all such deaths. The International Labor Organization says that half of workplace fatalities are avoidable. In *A Job to Die For*, Lisa Cullen writes:

In the workplace, few real accidents occur because the surroundings and operations are known; therefore, hazards can be identified. When harm from those hazards can be foreseen, accidents can be prevented....

Most jobs have expected, known hazards. Working in and near excavations, for example, poses the obvious risks of death or injury from cave-in.... When trenches or excavations collapse because soil was piled right up to the edge, there is little room to claim it was an accident. ⌷

38
THE SUICIDE RATE IS HIGHEST AMONG THE ELDERLY

If you judge by the media and the public education programs, you might be inclined to think that teenagers and young adults (aged 15 to 24) are the age group most likely to kill themselves. Actually, they have the second-*lowest* rate of suicide. (The absolute lowest rate is among kids aged 5 to 14; children younger than that are apparently deemed incapable of consciously choosing to end their lives.) It is the elderly, by far, who have the highest rate of suicide.

In the US, of every 100,000 people aged 75 to 79, 16.5 kill themselves. For those 80 and over, the rate is 19.43. This compares to a rate of 8.15 per 100,000 for people between the ages of 15 and 19, and 12.84 for people aged 20 to 24.

As with every age group, men are far more likely to kill themselves, but among the elderly this trend reaches extreme proportions. Of people 65 and older, men comprise a staggering 84 percent of suicides.

Because men commit the vast majority of *hara-kiri* among old people, looking at these male suicide rates makes for extremely depressing reading. For guys aged 75 to 79, the suicide rate is 34.26 per 100,000. In the 80 to 84 group, men's suicide rate is 44.12. When you look at men 85 and older, the suicide rate is a heart-breaking 54.52. Compare this to the suicide rate for dudes in their mid to late teens: 13.22 per 100,000.

It is true that suicide ranks as the second or third most common cause of death in young people (depending on age group), while it is number 15 and under for various groups of the elderly. Still, the suicide rate among the young is equal to their proportion of the population, while the elderly are way overrepresented as a group. And old people are cut down by a great many diseases and disorders virtually unknown to the young, which naturally pushes suicide down in the rankings.

The reasons why this suicide epidemic is ignored are highly speculative and would be too lengthy to get into here. However, we can rule out one seemingly likely explanation — suicide among the aged is invisible because they usually O.D. on prescription drugs or kill themselves in other ways that could easily be mistaken for natural death in someone of advanced years. This doesn't wash, primarily because guns are the most common method of dispatch. Of suicides over 65, men used a gun 79.5 percent of the time, while women shot themselves 37 percent of the time. It's hard to mistake that for natural causes.

The sky-high suicide rate among the elderly applies to the entire world, not just the US. Plotted in a graph, suicide rates by age group around the globe gently curve upward as age increases. When the graph reaches the final age group, the line suddenly spikes, especially for men. Worldwide, men 75 and over have a suicide rate of 55.7 per 100,000, while women in the same age group have a rate of 18.8. This rate for old men is almost three times the global rate for guys aged 15 to 24, while the rate for old women is well over three times the rate for young gals in that age group. ⌕

39
FOR LOW-RISK PEOPLE, A POSITIVE RESULT FROM AN HIV TEST IS WRONG HALF THE TIME

Although a lot of progress has been made in improving the length and quality of life for people with AIDS, getting a positive result from an HIV test must still rank as one of the worst pieces of news a person can get. It's not uncommon for people to kill themselves right after hearing the results, and those who don't commit suicide surely go through all kinds of mental anguish. But the accuracy of these tests is lower than generally believed. In fact, if you test positive but you're not a member of a high-risk group (such as non-monogamous gay men and intravenous drug users), the odds are 50-50 that you actually have the virus.

To be declared HIV-positive, your blood goes through three tests — two ELISA tests and one more sensitive and costly Western Blot test. Makers of the tests trumpet a 99.99 percent accuracy rate when all three are used. Many AIDS counselors even tell people that the tests *never* give a false positive (that is, the tests don't indicate that someone is HIV-positive when he or she really isn't). The test manufacturers' claim is misleading, and the counselors' claim is flat-out BS. Cognitive scientist Gerd Gigerenzer — who specializes in risk and uncertainty — explains the reality in plain English:

Imagine 10,000 men who are not in any known risk category. One is infected (base rate) and will test positive with practical certainty (sensitivity). Of the 9,999 men who are not infected, another one will also test positive (false positive rate). So we can expect that two men will test positive.

Out of these two men, only one actually carries the virus. So, if you're a low-risk man who tests positive, the chances are even — the same as a coin flip — that the result is right. It's highly advisable that you take the tests again (and again). The results are even less reliable for women in low-risk groups, since they have a still lower rate of HIV.

Of course, this doesn't apply to an HIV-negative result. If you test negative, the odds are overwhelmingly good (9,998 out of 9,999) that this is correct. It also doesn't hold for people in high-risk categories. For example, if we accept the estimate that 1.5 percent of gay men are HIV-positive, this means that out of every 10,000, an average of 150 are infected. An HIV test will almost surely pick up on all 150, and out of the remaining 9,850 uninfected men, one will incorrectly be labeled positive. This means that only one out of 151 gay men will be falsely diagnosed as having HIV. A false positive is thus still possible but much more unlikely. ⟳

40
DNA MATCHING IS NOT INFALLIBLE

Speaking of tests that aren't all they're cracked up to be, let's look at DNA testing. This is supposed to be the absolute silver bullet of criminal justice, an incontrovertible way to pin guilt on someone. After all, the chances of a mismatch are one in a billion, a quadrillion, a jillion! Some experts have testified under oath that a false match is literally impossible.

Not quite. As he did with HIV testing, risk scholar Gerd Gigerenzer of the Max Planck Institute punches a hole in the matching of genetic material:

In the first blind test reported in the literature, three major commercial laboratories were each sent 50 DNA samples. Two of the three declared one false match; in a second test one year later, one of the same three laboratories declared a false match. From external tests conducted by the California Association of Crime Laboratory Directors, the Collaborative Testing Services, and other agencies, the psychologist Jonathan Koehler and his colleagues estimated the false positive rate of DNA fingerprinting to be on the order of 1 in 100. Cellmark Diagnostics, one of the laboratories that found matches between O.J. Simpson's DNA and DNA extracted from a recovered blood stain at the murder scene, reported its own false positive rate to the Simpson defense as roughly 1 in 200.

It gets even worse. In 1999, the College of American Pathologists performed its own secret tests of 135 labs. Each lab was sent a DNA sample from the "victim," some semen from the "suspect," and a fake vaginal swab containing DNA from both parties. They were also sent a strand of the "victim's" hair. The object was to see how many of the labs would make the matches (ie, match the two sperm samples of the man, and match the hair and DNA sample of the woman). But something unexpected happened: Three of the labs reported that the DNA from the suspect matched the victim's DNA! Obviously, they had mixed up the samples. Only fourteen labs tested the hair, but out of those, one screwed it up by declaring a match to the "suspect."

These kind of switches don't happen only during artificial situations designed to gauge a lab's accuracy (which are usually performed under ideal conditions). During a 1995 rape trial, a lab reversed the labels on the DNA samples from the victim and the defendant. Their testing then revealed a match between the defendant's alleged DNA (which was actually the victim's) and the

DNA on the vaginal swab, which didn't contain any semen from the rapist. Luckily, this boneheaded move was caught during the trial, but not everyone is so lucky.

The *Journal of Forensic Science* has reported an error that was discovered only after an innocent man had been convicted of raping an 11-year-old girl and sentenced to prison, where he was undoubtedly brutalized in ways that would give you nightmares for the rest of your life, were you to hear them described in detail. After four years, he was released because the lab hadn't completely separated the real rapist's DNA (extracted from his semen) from the victim's DNA. When the two were swirled together, they somehow matched that of the poor bastard whose eleven alibi witnesses failed to sway the jury. But when the semen DNA was checked properly, it was beyond doubt that a match didn't exist.

While most false matches are the result of human error, other factors do come into play. Some testing techniques are more definitive than others. In the case of one innocent man — Josiah Sutton, found guilty of rape based primarily on DNA evidence — criminology professor William C. Thompson said: "If police picked any two black men off the street, the chances that one of them would have a DNA profile that 'matched' the semen sample as well as Sutton's profile is better than one in eight." Also, we mustn't forget about corruption. In some known cases, DNA analysts have misrepresented (ie, lied about) their findings in order to obtain convictions. ⌑

41

AN FBI EXPERT TESTIFIED THAT LIE DETECTORS ARE WORTHLESS FOR SECURITY SCREENING

Now let's turn our attention to the last member of our trifecta of defective tests — the polygraph, more commonly referred to as the lie detector. Invented by the same person who created Wonder Woman and her golden lasso that makes you tell the truth (I'm not kidding), the polygraph is said to detect deception based on subtle bodily signals, such as pulse rate and sweatiness. Its proponents like to claim that it has a success rate of 90 percent or more. This is pure hogwash. While the evidence against lie detectors is way too voluminous to get into here, it will be very instructive to look at a statement from Dr. Drew Richardson. Richardson is a scientist who was an FBI agent for 25 years; in the late 1980s and early 1990s, he dealt with polygraphs.

In fall 1997, a Senate Judiciary subcommittee held hearings regarding the FBI Crime Lab. Richardson gave scorching testimony about polygraphs. Referring specifically to the practice of using lie detectors to question people in sensitive positions, he said under oath:

It is completely without any theoretical foundation and has absolutely no validity. Although there is disagreement amongst scientists about the use of polygraph testing in criminal matters, there is almost universal agreement that polygraph screening is completely invalid and should be stopped. As one of my colleagues frequently says, the diagnostic value of this type of testing is no more than that of astrology or tea-leaf reading.

If this test had any validity (which it does not), both my own experience, and published scientific research has proven, that anyone can be taught to beat this type of polygraph exam in a few minutes.

Because of the nature of this type of examination, it would normally be expected to produce large numbers of false positive results (falsely accusing an examinee of lying about some issue). As a result of the great consequences of doing this with large numbers of law enforcement and intelligence community officers, the test has now been manipulated to reduce false positive results, but consequently has no power to detect deception in espionage and other national security matters. Thus, I believe that there is virtually no probability of catching a spy with the use of polygraph screening techniques. I think a careful examination of the Aldrich Ames case will reveal that any shortcomings in the use of the polygraph were not simply errors on the part of the polygraph examiners involved, and would not have been eliminated if FBI instead of CIA polygraphers had conducted these examinations. Instead I believe this is largely a reflection of the complete lack of validity of this methodology. To the extent that we place any confidence in the results of polygraph screening, and as a consequence shortchange traditional security vetting techniques, I think our national security is severely jeopardized.

After he ripped polygraphs a new one, the FBI silenced Richardson, refusing to let him speak publicly about the subject again. 🖰

42
THE BAYER COMPANY MADE HEROIN

Aspirin isn't the only "wonder drug that works wonders" that Bayer made. The German pharmaceutical giant also introduced heroin to the world.

The company was looking for a cough suppressant that didn't have problematic side effects, mainly addiction, like morphine and codeine. And if it could relieve pain better than morphine, that was a welcome bonus.

When one of Bayer's chemists approached the head of the pharmacological lab with ASA — to be sold under the name "aspirin" — he was waved away. The boss was more interested in something else the chemists had cooked up — diacetyl-morphine. (This narcotic had been created in 1874 by a British chemist, who had never done anything with it.)

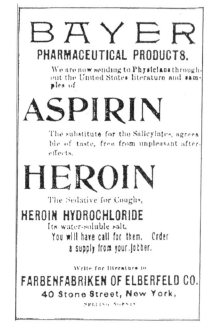

Using the tradename "Heroin" — because early testers said it made them feel *heroisch* (heroic) — Bayer sold this popular drug by the truckload starting in 1898. Free samples were sent to thousands of doctors; studies appeared in medical journals. The *Sunday Times* of London noted: "By 1899, Bayer was producing about a ton of heroin a year, and exporting the drug to 23 countries," including the US. Medicines containing smack were available over-the-counter at drug stores, just as aspirin is today. The American Medical Association gave heroin its stamp of approval in 1907.

But reports of addiction, which had already started appearing in 1899, turned into a torrent after several years. Bayer had wisely released aspirin the year after heroin, and this new non-addictive painkiller and anti-inflammatory was well on its way to becoming the most popular drug ever. In 1913, Bayer got out of the heroin business.

Not that the company has kept its nose clean since then:

A division of the pharmaceutical company Bayer sold millions of dollars of blood-clotting medicine for hemophiliacs — medicine that carried a high risk of transmitting AIDS — to Asia and Latin America in the mid-1980s while selling a new, safer product in the West, according to documents obtained by *The New York Times*.... [I]n Hong Kong and Taiwan alone, more than 100 hemophiliacs got HIV after using Cutter's old medicine, according to records and interviews. Many have since died. ▯

43
LSD HAS BEEN USED SUCCESSFULLY IN PSYCHIATRIC THERAPY

Given the demonization of the psychedelic drug LSD, it may seem inconceivable that mainstream psychiatrists were giving it to patients during sessions. Yet for at least 20 years, that's exactly what happened.

Created in 1938, LSD was first suggested as a tool in psychotherapy in 1949. The following year saw the first studies in medical/psychiatric journals. By 1970, hundreds of articles on the uses of LSD in therapy had appeared in the *Journal of the American Medical Association*, the *Journal of Psychology*, the *Archives of General Psychiatry*, the *Quarterly Journal of Studies of Alcoholism*, many non-English-language journals, and elsewhere.

Psychiatric and psychotherapeutic conferences had segments devoted to LSD, and two professional organizations were formed for this specialty, one in Europe and the other in North America. International symposia were held in Princeton, London, Amsterdam, and other locations. From 1950 to 1965, LSD was given in conjunction with therapy to an estimated 40,000 people worldwide.

In his definitive book on the subject, *LSD Psychotherapy*, transpersonal psychotherapist Stanislav Grof, MD, explains what makes LSD such a good aid to headshrinking:

...LSD and other psychedelics function more or less as nonspecific catalysts and

amplifiers of the psyche.... In the dosages used in human experimentation, the classical psychedelics, such as LSD, psilocybin, and mescaline, do not have any specific pharmacological effects. They increase the energetic niveau in the psyche and the body which leads to manifestation of otherwise latent psychological processes.

The content and nature of the experiences that these substances induce are thus not artificial products of their pharmacological interaction with the brain ("toxic psychoses"), but authentic expressions of the psyche revealing its functioning on levels not ordinarily available for observation and study. A person who has taken LSD does not have an "LSD experience," but takes a journey into deep recesses of his or her own psyche.

When used as a tool during full-scale therapy, Grof says, "the potential of LSD seems to be extraordinary and unique. The ability of LSD to deepen, intensify and accelerate the psychotherapeutic process is incomparably greater than that of any other drug used as an adjunct to psychotherapy, with the exception perhaps of some other members of the psychedelic group."

Due to bad trips experienced by casual users, not to mention anti-drug hysteria in general, LSD was outlawed in the US in 1970. The Drug Enforcement Agency declares: "Scientific study of LSD ceased circa 1980 as research funding declined."

What the DEA fails to mention is that medical and psychiatric research is currently happening, albeit quietly. Few researchers have the resources and patience to jump through the umpteen hoops required to test psychedelics on people, but a few experiments using LSD, ecstasy, DMT, ketamine, peyote, and other such substances are happening in North America and Europe. Universities engaged in this research include Harvard, Duke, Johns Hopkins, University College London, and the University of Zurich.

We're presently in the dark ages of such research, but at least the light hasn't gone out entirely. ¤

44
CARL SAGAN WAS AN AVID POT-SMOKER

When you're talking about scientists who achieved rock-star status in the second half of the twentieth century, the late astronomer and biologist Carl Sagan is right up there with Stephen Hawking. His *Cosmos* (1980) is one of the most popular science books ever written, planting itself on the *New York Times* bestseller list for 70 weeks and staying perpetually in print ever since. It was a companion for the PBS television series of the same name, which — along with numerous *Tonight Show* appearances — introduced Sagan and his emphatically stated phrase "billions and billions" into pop culture. His sole novel, *Contact*, was turned into a love-it-or-hate-it movie starring Jodie Foster as an erstwhile scientist searching for extraterrestrial life, with Matthew McConaughey as a New Age flake who, inevitably, makes his own form of contact with her.

Besides his pop-culture credentials, Sagan was pals with numerous legendary Nobel Prize-winners while still in college, picked up a Pulitzer Prize for his book *Dragons of Eden*, and consulted for NASA, MIT, Cornell, and RAND. He designed the human race's postcards to any aliens that might be out there — the plaque onboard the *Pioneer* space probes and the record on the *Voyager* probes.

So it might come as a bit of a surprise that Sagan was an avid smoker of marijuana. Some might even call him a pothead.

In his definitive biography of the celebrity scientist, Keay Davidson reveals that Sagan started toking regularly in the early 1960s and that *Dragons of Eden* — which won the Pulitzer — "was obviously written under the inspiration of marijuana." Davidson says of Sagan:

He believed the drug enhanced his creativity and insights. His closest friend of three decades, Harvard psychiatry professor Dr. Lester Grinspoon, a leading advocate of the decriminalization of marijuana, recalls an incident in the 1980s when one of his California admirers mailed him, unsolicited, some unusually high-quality pot. Grinspoon shared the joints with Sagan and his wife, Anne Druyan. Afterward, Sagan said, "Lester, I know you've only got one left, but could I have it? I've got serious work to do tomorrow and I could really use it."

Perhaps letting Sagan bogart the pot was Grinspoon's way of returning a favor, since Sagan had contributed an essay to *Marihuana Reconsidered*, Grinspoon's classic 1971 book on the benefits and low risks of reefer. For almost three decades, the author of this ode to Mary Jane was anonymous, but in 1999 Grinspoon revealed that "Mr. X" was Sagan.

In the essay, Sagan wrote that weed increased his appreciation of art, music, food, sex, and childhood memories, and gave him insights into scientific and social matters:

I can remember one occasion, taking a shower with my wife while high, in which I had an idea on the origins and invalidities of racism in terms of Gaussian distribution curves. It was a point obvious [sic] in a way, but rarely talked about. I drew curves in soap on the shower wall, and went to write the idea down. One idea led to another, and at the end of about an hour of extremely hard work I found I had written eleven short essays on a wide range of social, political, philosophical, and human biological topics…. I have used them in university commencement addresses, public lectures, and in my books.

The staunchly atheistic/humanistic Sagan comes perilously close to mysticism in some passages:

I do not consider myself a religious person in the usual sense, but there is a religious aspect to some highs. The heightened sensitivity in all areas gives me a feeling of communion with my surroundings, both animate and inanimate. Sometimes a kind of existential perception of the absurd comes over me and I see with awful certainty the hypocrisies and posturing of myself and my fellow

men. And at other times, there is a different sense of the absurd, a playful and whimsical awareness....

I am convinced that there are genuine and valid levels of perception available with cannabis (and probably with other drugs) which are, through the defects of our society and our educational system, unavailable to us without such drugs. Such a remark applies not only to self-awareness and to intellectual pursuits, but also to perceptions of real people, a vastly enhanced sensitivity to facial expression, intonations, and choice of words which sometimes yields a rapport so close it's as if two people are reading each other's minds.

45
ONE OF THE HEROES OF *BLACK HAWK DOWN* IS A CONVICTED CHILD MOLESTER

The movie *Black Hawk Down* was one of the biggest box office draws of 2001, and it earned its director, Ridley Scott, an Oscar nomination. (He didn't win, but the movie got two Academy Awards for editing and sound.) Based on Mark Bowden's nonfiction book of the same title, it concerns the disastrous raid of Mogadishu, Somalia, by US elite soldiers in 1993.

One of these Special Forces soldiers underwent a name-change as he moved from the printed page to the big screen. Ranger John "Stebby" Stebbins became Ranger Danny Grimes when played by Scottish heartthrob Ewan McGregor. Why? Because in 2000, Stebbins was court-martialed and sent to the stockade for rape and sodomy of a child under twelve.

This decidedly unheroic turn of events was confirmed by the Army, the Fort Leavenworth military prison (Stebby's home for the next 30 years), and *Black Hawk Down*'s author. Bowden told the *New York Post* that the Army asked him to change Stebbins' name in the screenplay in order to avoid embarrassing the military.

In an email to the newspaper, Stebby's ex-wife, Nora Stebbins, wrote: "They are going to make millions off this film in which my ex-husband is portrayed as an All-American hero when the truth is he is not." ⌨

46
THE AUTO INDUSTRY SAYS THAT SUV DRIVERS ARE SELFISH AND INSECURE

People who tool around in hulking, big-ass sport utility vehicles have been getting dissed a lot lately, but no one has raked them over the coals like the people who sold them the SUVs in the first place. The multibillion-dollar auto industry does extensive research into its customers, and lately that research has focused quite a bit on the people who buy SUVs.

Investigative reporter Keith Bradsher of the *New York Times* has looked into the SUV phenomenon for years. He's read marketing reports meant only to be seen within the industry; he's interviewed marketing executives from the car companies and from outside research firms.

The industry has come to some unflattering conclusions about the people who buy its SUVs. As summarized by Bradsher:

They tend to be people who are insecure and vain. They are frequently nervous about their marriages and uncomfortable about parenthood. They often lack confidence in their driving skills. Above all, they are apt to be self-centered and self-absorbed, with little interest in their neighbors and communities....

They are more restless, more sybaritic, and less social than most Americans are. They tend to like fine restaurants a lot more than off-road driving, seldom go to church and have limited interest in doing volunteer work to help others.

David Bostwick, the director of market research at Chrysler, told Bradsher: "We have a basic resistance in our society to admitting that we are parents, and no longer able to go out and find another mate. If you have a sport utility, you can have the smoked windows, put the children in the back and pretend you're still single."

Bostwick says that compared to those who buy similarly large minivans, SUV drivers are selfish:

Sport utility people say, "I already have two kids, I don't need 20." Then we talk to the people who have minivans and they say, "I don't have two kids, I have 20 — all the kids in the neighborhood."

One of General Motors' top engineers also spoke of the difference between minivanners and

SUVers: "SUV owners want to be more like, 'I'm in control of the people around me.'" He went on:

With the sport utility buyers, it's more of an image thing. Sport utility buyers tend to be more like, "I wonder how people view me," and are more willing to trade off flexibility or functionality to get that.

The executive VP for North American auto operations at Honda revealed: "The people who buy SUVs are in many cases buying the outside first and then the inside. They are buying the image of the SUV first, and then the functionality."

Jim Bulin, a former Ford strategist who started his own marketing firm, told Bradsher: "It's about not letting anything get in your way and, in the extreme, about intimidating others to get out of your way." Daniel A. Gorell, who also used to market for Ford and now has his own firm, says simply that SUV drivers are "less giving, less oriented toward others."

Defenders of SUVs have attacked Bradsher for reporting these things, but they always forget the crucial point: Bradsher isn't the one slamming SUV owners — it's the auto industry itself. ⌑

47
THE WORD "SQUAW" IS NOT A DERISIVE TERM FOR THE VAGINA

It's widely believed that "squaw" is a crude word for the vagina. Whether people under this misapprehension believe that the word is Native American (specifically from the Mohawk language) or was made up by Europeans, they think that calling a woman "squaw" is the same as calling her "cunt." Activists are on a crusade to stamp out the word, which is part of over 1,000 placenames in the United States, and they've met with some success. A 1995 Minnesota law, for example, ordered the changing of all geographical names containing the misunderstood word.

William Bright — UCLA professor emeritus of linguistics and anthropology, and editor of the book *Native American Placenames of the United States* — writes:

All linguists who have commented on the word "squaw," including specialists on Indian languages and on the history of American vocabulary, agree that it is not from Mohawk, or any other Iroquoian language. Rather, the word was borrowed as early as 1624 from Massachusett, the language of Algonquians in the area we now call Massachusetts; in that language it meant simply "young woman."

Several languages of the Algonquian family — including Cree, Objibwa, and Fox — still use similar words for "woman."

The confusion might have come from the fact that the Mohawk word for a woman's naughty bits is "otsískwa." But since Mohawk belongs to a different language family (Iroquois), the etymologies of the words are completely separate. Bright notes that current speakers of Mohawk don't consider "squaw" in any way related to their word for vagina.

Still, there is no doubt that "squaw" has been used as an epithet by white people, starting at least in the 1800s. It even appears this way in the work of James Fenimore Cooper. However, given its meaning of "woman," when used in a mean-spirited way, it's probably more equivalent to "broad" or "bitch" than to "cunt." Even this is a corruption of the word's true definition.

The many places across the US with names incorporating "squaw" were labeled that way to *honor* female chiefs or other outstanding Native women, or because women performed traditional activities at these locations. In an essay that earned her death threats, Abenaki storyteller and historical consultant Marge Bruchac wrote:

Any word can hurt when used as a weapon. Banning the word will not erase the past, and will only give the oppressors power to define our language. What words will be next? Pappoose? Sachem? Pow Wow? If we accept the slander, and internalize the insult, we discredit our female ancestors who felt no shame at hearing the word spoken. To ban indigenous words discriminates against Native people and their languages. Are we to be condemned to speaking only the "King's English?" What about all the words from other Native American languages?....

When I hear it ["squaw"] spoken by Native peoples, in its proper context, I hear the voices of the ancestors. I am reminded of powerful grandmothers who nurtured our people and fed the strangers, of proud women chiefs who stood up against them, and of mothers and daughters and sisters who still stand here today. ♡

48
YOU CAN MAIL LETTERS FOR LITTLE OR NO COST

I may never receive another piece of mail, but I have to let you in on a secret: It's possible to send letters for free or for well below current postage rates. Information on beating the postal system has been floating around for decades, but it wasn't gathered in one place until outlaw publisher Loompanics put forth *How To Screw the Post Office* by "Mr. Unzip" in 2000.

Not content to theorize from an ivory tower, Unzip put these methods through the ultimate real-world test: He mailed letters. He also examined the envelopes in which hundreds upon hundreds of customers had paid their utility bills. Based on this, he offers proof that letters with insufficient postage often make it to their destinations.

The key is that the machines which scan for stamps work incredibly fast, processing ten letters per second. They're also fairly unsophisticated in their detection methods, relying mainly on stamps' glossy coating as a signal. Because of this, it's possible to successfully use lower-rate stamps, including outdated stamps, postcard stamps, and even 1-cent stamps. Beyond that, Unzip successfully sent letters affixed with only the perforated edges from a block of stamps. Even those pseudostamps sent by charities like Easter Seals or environmental groups can fool the scanners.

Another approach is to cut stamps in half, using each portion as full postage. Not only does this give you two stamps for the price of one, but you can often salvage the uncancelled portion of stamps on letters you receive. In fact, the author shows that sometimes the Post Office processes stamps that have already been fully cancelled. This happens more often when the ink is light, but even dark cancellation marks aren't necessarily a deal-breaker.

Then there's the biggie, the Post Office's atomic secret that lets you mail letters for free. Say you're sending a letter to dear old mom. Simply put mom's address as the return address. Then write your address in the center of the envelope, where you'd normally put hers. Forget about the stamp. The letter will be "returned" to her for insufficient postage.

Unzip covers further techniques involving stamp positioning, metered mail, 2-cent stamps, and other tricks. Except perhaps for the reversed address scam, none of these tricks will guarantee your missive gets to its destination, so you wouldn't want to try them with important letters. But if you want to save a few cents once in a while — or more likely, you want to have fun hacking the postal system — it can be done. ▢

49
ADVERTISERS' INFLUENCE ON THE NEWS MEDIA IS WIDESPREAD

In 1995, the *San Jose Mercury News* almost went under because of a boycott by all of its car company advertisers. Why were they so irate? The *Merc* had published an article telling consumers how to negotiate a better price with car dealers.

When the executive editor of the *Chicago Sun-Times*, Larry Green, was challenged for displaying editorial favoritism toward advertisers, he openly declared: "We have to take care of our customers."

Tales like this bubble up every once in a while, so it shouldn't come as a shock that advertisers sometimes try to influence the news outlets that run their ads. The real shock is how often this happens.

In its 2002 survey, the Project for Excellence in Journalism asked 103 local TV newsrooms across the US about pressure from sponsors:

In all, 17 percent of news directors say that sponsors have discouraged them from pursuing stories (compared to 18 percent last year), and 54 percent have been pressured to cover stories about sponsors, up slightly from 47 percent last year.

Of the stations that investigated auto companies that were sponsors, half suffered economically for it, usually by the withdrawal of advertising. One car company cancelled $1 million of ads it had planned with a station.

In a classic 1992 survey (that desperately needs to be repeated), Marquette University's Department of Journalism tallied questionnaire results from 147 editors of daily newspapers. Among the findings:

■ 93.2 percent said sponsors had "threatened to withdraw advertising from [the] paper because of the content of the stories." (89 percent replied that the advertisers followed through on this threat.)

■ 89.9 percent responded that advertisers had "tried to influence the content of a news story or feature."

■ 36.7 percent said that advertisers had "succeeded in influencing news or features in [the] newspaper."

■ 71.4 percent said that "an advertiser tried to kill a story at [the] newspaper."

■ 55.1 percent revealed that they had gotten "pressure from within [the] paper to write or tailor news stories to please advertisers."

In the decade since this poll, the media have become even more corporate and more consolidated, so it's hard to imagine that the situation has improved. ロ

50
THE WORLD'S MUSEUMS CONTAIN INNUMERABLE FAKES

The next time you're marveling at a painting by Picasso, a statue by Michelangelo, or a carving from ancient Egypt, don't be absolutely sure that you're looking at the genuine article. Art fakery has been around since ancient times and is still in full swing — museums, galleries, and private collections around the world are stocked with phonies. This fact comes to us from an insider's insider — Thomas Hoving, former director of the Metropolitan Museum of Art in New York City. In his book *False Impressions: The Hunt for Big-Time Art Fakes*, he writes:

The fact is that there are so many phonies and doctored pieces around these days that at times, I almost believe that there are as many bogus works as genuine ones. In the decade and a half that I was with the Metropolitan Museum of Art I must have examined fifty thousand works in all fields. Fully 40 percent were either phonies or so hypocritically restored or so misattributed that they were just the same as forgeries. Since then I'm sure that that percentage has risen. What few art professionals seem to want to admit is that the art world we are living in today is a new, highly active, unprincipled one of art fakery.

Ancient Egyptian objects are particularly likely to be bogus. Furthermore, Hoving estimates that the fraud rate for religious artifacts from pagan and early Christian times is literally 99 percent. As many as 5,000 fake Dürers were created after the master's death, and half of Vienna master Egon Schiele's pencil drawings are fakes.

But it isn't just current con artists making this junk; the ancients did it, too. For around a millennia, Romans couldn't get enough of Greek statues, gems, glasses, and other objects, so forgers stepped in to fill the demand. Hoving writes:

The volume was so great that Seneca the Elder (ca. 55 BC – AD 39) is recorded by a contemporaneous historian as remarking that there were no fewer than half a dozen workshops in the first century AD working full time in Rome on just colored gems and intaglios. Today it's almost impossible to tell what's genuinely ancient Greek and what's Roman fakery, because those gems and intaglios are made of material that dates to ancient times and the style is near perfect.

Art forgery isn't the realm of nobodies, either. During certain periods of their lives, Renaissance masters Donatello and Verochio put bread on the table by creating *faux* antiquities. Rubens painted copies of earlier artists. El Greco's assistants created five or six copies of their boss' work, each of which was then passed off as the original (and they're still wrongly considered the originals).

Hoving reveals that pretty much every museum has at one time or another been suckered into buying and displaying fakes, and many are still showing them. Of course, most of the examples he uses are from the Met, but he also says that phony works still sit in the Louvre, the Getty, the British Museum, the Museum of Fine Arts, Boston, and the Vatican, among others. (Hoving estimates that 90 percent of the ancient Roman statues in the Holy See's collection are actually eighteenth-century European knock-offs.)

Revealing further examples, the *Independent* of London catalogs three Goyas in the Met that are now attributed to other artists; Rodin sketches actually done by his mistress; Fragonard's popular *Le baiser à la dérobée* (*The Stolen Kiss*), which seems to have been painted by his sister-in-law; and many Rubens works actually created by the artist's students. According to the newspaper: "The Rembrandt Research Committee claims that most works attributed to Rembrandt were in fact collaborative studio pieces."

It's enough to make you question the ceiling of the Sistine Chapel. ▢

REFERENCES

Ten Commandments. Book of Exodus, King James Bible.

Pope's Erotic Book. Piccolomini, Aeneas Silvius (Pius II). *The Goodli History of the Ladye Lucres of Scene and of Her Lover Eurialus*. Edited by E.J. Morrall. Oxford University Press, 1996. • Website of James O'Donnell, former professor of classical studies at the University of Pennsylvania [ccat.sas.upenn.edu/jod/]. • Translations from early English into modern English by Russ Kick.

CIA Crimes. Kelly, John. "Crimes and Silence." *Into the Buzzsaw: Leading Journalists Expose the Myth of a Free Press*. Edited by Kristina Borjesson. Amherst, NY: Prometheus Books, 2002, pp 311-31. • Permanent Select Committee on Intelligence, US House of Representatives, 104th Congress. "IC21: The Intelligence Community in the 21st Century." Government Printing Office, 1996, chapter 9: "Clandestine Service."

CIA Agent. Gup, Ted. *The Book of Honor: Covert Lives and Classified Deaths at the CIA*. Doubleday (Random House), 2000. • Further reading: Laird, Thomas. *Into Tibet: The CIA's First Atomic Spy and His Secret Expedition to Lhasa*. Grove Press, 2002.

Afghanistan's Food Supply. Woodward, Bob, and Dan Balz. "Combating Terrorism: 'It Starts Today.'" ("10 Days in September," part 6). *Washington Post*, 1 Feb 2002. • This revelation was first unburied by Matthew Rothschild, editor of *The Progressive*.

Terrorism Convictions. Fazlollah, Mark. "Reports of Terror Crimes Inflated." *Philadelphia Inquirer*, 15 May 2003. • Fazlollah, Mark, and Peter Nicholas. "US Overstates Arrests in Terrorism." *Philadelphia Inquirer*, 16 Dec 2001. • United States General Accounting Office. "Justice Department: Better Management Oversight and Internal Controls Needed to Ensure Accuracy of Terrorism-Related Statistics." Jan 2003.

Provoking Terrorist Attack. Arkin, William M. "The Secret War." *Los Angeles Times*, 27 Oct 2002. • Defense Science Board. "DBS Summer Study on Special Operations and Joint Forces in Support of Counter Terrorism, Final Outbrief," 16 Aug 2002 (declassified version). • Floyd, Chris. "Global Eye -- Into the Dark." *Moscow Times*, 1 Nov 2002. • Hess, Pamela. "Panel Wants $7bn Elite Counter-terror Unit." United Press International, 26 Sept 2002.

Nuking the Moon. Barnett, Antony. "US Planned One Big Nuclear Blast for Mankind." *Observer* (London), 14 May 2000. • Davidson, Keay. *Carl Sagan: A Life. New York*: John Wiley & Sons, 1999. • Ulivi, Paolo. "Nuke the Moon!" Grand Tour Planetary Exploration Page [utenti.lycos.it/paoloulivi/], 13 Oct 2002. Ulivi is an engineer and the author of an upcoming book on unmanned lunar exploration from Springer-Praxis Publishing Ltd. • Zabarenko, Deborah. "Moon Bomb?" Reuters News Agency, 17 May 2000. • Zheleznyakov, Aleksandr. "The E-4 Project: Exploding a Nuclear Bomb on the Moon."

Enciklopediya Kosmonavtika [Cosmonautics Encyclopedia]. Translated by Sven Grahn of the Swedish Space Corporation [www.svengrahn.pp.se/ histind/E3/E3orig.htm].

Nuking North Carolina. The Goldsboro incident remained shrouded in mystery and misinformation until four students at the University of North Carolina at Chapel Hill did loads of original research (interviews, FOIA requests, etc.) and created a Website called Broken Arrow: Goldsboro, NC <www.ibiblio.org/bomb/>. It is by far the definitive source of information on this almost-catastrophe. The students are Cliff Nelson, Nick Harrison, Andrew Leung, and Megan E. Butler.

World War III. Kozlov, Yuriy, and Aleksandr Stepanenko. "Norwegian Rocket Incident Settled." ITAR-TASS (Moscow), 27 Jan 1995. • Krieger, David. "Crisis and Opportunity." Website of the Nuclear Age Peace Foundation [www.wagingpeace.org], 2002. • The Back From the Brink Campaign. *Short Fuse to Catastrophe: The Case for Taking Nuclear Weapons Off Hair-trigger Alert* (briefing book). Self-published, 2001, p 4. [www.backfromthebrink.org].

Korean War Never Ended. Hermes, Walter. "Armistice Negotiations." *The Korean War: An Encyclopedia*. Ed. by Stanley Sandler. Garland Publishing, 1995. • Levie, Howard S. "Armistice." *Crimes of War: What the Public Should Know*. Ed. by Roy Gutman and David Rieff. W.W. Norton & Co., 1999. • Text of the Korean War Armistice Agreement, 27 July 1953. • Unsigned. "The Korean War Armistice." BBC News, 18 Feb 2003.

Agent Orange in Korea. "Agent Orange and Related Issues." Department of Veterans Affairs Fact Sheet, Jan 2003. • "Agent Orange Outside of Viet Nam." *News and Notes for Florida Veterans*, Apr 2003. Department of Veterans Affairs, St. Petersburg Regional Office. • Jelinek, Pauline. "Some to Get Agent Orange Testing." Associated Press, 3 Nov 2000. • VHA Directive 2000-027: Registry Examinations for Veterans Possibly Exposed to Agent Orange in Korea. Department of Veterans Affairs, Veterans Health Administration, 5 Sept 2000.

Student Massacres. Cabell, Brian, and Matt Smith. "S.C. College Marks 'Orangeburg Massacre' Anniversary." CNN, 8 Feb 2001. • Sellers, Cleveland. "The Orangeburg Massacre, 1968." *It Did Happen Here: Recollections of Political Repression in America*. Ed. by Bud Schultz and Ruth Schultz. University of California Press, 1989. • Spofford, Tim. Lynch Street: *The May 1970 Slayings at Jackson State College*. Kent State University Press, 1988. • "The May 1970 Tragedy at Jackson State University." Jackson State University Website. [http://www.jsums.edu/~www/gg02.htm]. • Further reading: Nelson, Jack, and Jack Bass. *The Orangeburg Massacre* (second edition). Mercer University Press, 1999.

Churchill. Churchill, Winston. "Zionism Versus Bolshevism: A Struggle for the Soul of the Jewish People." *Illustrated Sunday Herald* (London), 8 Feb 1920. An image of the original article as it was printed has been widely reproduced on the Web. • "Sir Winston Churchill." Biography on the BBC Website. • Woods, Frederick. *A Bibliography of the Works of Sir Winston Churchill, KG, OM, CH, MP*. University of Toronto Press, 1963: p 186.

REFERENCES

Auschwitz Tattoo. Black, Edwin. "The IBM Link to Auschwitz." *Village Voice*, 9 Oct 2002.

Hitler's Relatives. Gardner, David. *The Last of the Hitlers*. BMM, 2001. Gardner doesn't reveal the Hitlers' new last name nor the town in which they live.

Male Witches. Apps, Lara, and Andrew Gow. *Male Witches in Early Modern Europe*. Manchester University Press, 2003.

Cannibal Colonists. Zinn, Howard. *A People's History of the United States* (Perennial Classics Edition). HarperCollins Publishers, 2001, p 24. (Originally published 1980.)

Feminists Against Abortion. Taken directly from the writings of Anthony, Stanton, Blackwell, and Woodhull and Claflin, reproduced in MacNair, Rachel, Mare Krane Derr, and Linda Naranjo-Huebl (eds.). *Prolife Feminism: Yesterday and Today*. Sulzburger & Graham Publishing, 1995.

Black Confederates. Barrow, Charles Kelly, J.H. Segars, and R.B. Rosenburg. *Black Confederates*. Pelican Publishing Company, 2001. • Segars, J.H., and Charles Kelly Barrow. *Black Southerners in Confederate Armies: A Collection of Historical Accounts*. Southern Lion Books, 2001.

Electric Cars. Didik, Frank. "History and Directory of Electric Cars from 1834–1987." Didik Design Website [www.didik.com], 2001. • Rae, John B. "The Electric Vehicle Company: A Monopoly that Missed." *Business History Review*, 1955. • Schallenberg, Richard H. "Prospects for the Electric Vehicle: A Historical Perspective." *IEEE Transactions on Education*, vol. E-23, No 3, Aug 1980. • Schiffer, Michael Brian, with Tamara C. Butts and Kimberly K. Grimm. *Taking Charge: The Electric Automobile in America*. Smithsonian Institution Press, 1994. • Wakefield, Ernest Henry, PhD. *History of the Electric Automobile: Hybrid Electric Vehicles*. Society of Automotive Engineers, 1998.

Juries. Conrad, Clay S. *Jury Nullification: The Evolution of a Doctrine*. Carolina Academic Press, 1998. • Various literature from the Fully Informed Jury Association, [www.fija.org], 1-800-TEL-JURY, PO Box 5570, Helena MT 59604.

Police Nonprotection. Stevens, Richard W. *Dial 911 and Die: The Shocking Truth About the Police Protection Myth*. Mazel Freedom Press, 1999.

Government Can Take Your Home. Berliner, Dana. *Government Theft: Top 10 Abuses of Eminent Domain, 1998-2002*. Castle Coalition (a project of the Institute for Justice), 2003. • Berliner, Dana. *Public Power, Private Gain: A Five-Year, State-by-State Report Examining the Abuse of Eminent Domain*. Castle Coalition (a project of the Institute for Justice), Apr 2003.

Supreme Court on Drugs. Gray, Judge James P. *Why Our Drug Laws Have Failed and What We Can Do About It: A Judicial*

Indictment of the War on Drugs. Temple University Press, 2001. • *Linder v. United States*, 925. No. 183. U.S. Supreme Court 268 U.S. 5 (1925). • *Robinson v. California*. SCT.1193, 370 U.S. 660, 82 S. Ct. 1417, 8 L. Ed. 2d 758 (1962). • *Powell v. Texas*, 392 U.S. 514 (1968) (USSC).

Age of Consent. For the US, actual text of state laws. The Age of Consent Website [www.ageofconsent.com] contains all the relevant state codes, as well as links to the code on official state Websites. The site also has primarily official documentation (often from Interpol) regarding the laws in other countries.

Scientists' Citations. Muir, Hazel. "Scientists Exposed as Sloppy Reporters." *New Scientist*, 14 Dec 2002.

Pasteur. Waller, John. *Einstein's Luck: The Truth Behind Some of the Greatest Scientific Discoveries*. Oxford University Press, 2002: Chapter 1, "The Pasteurization of Spontaneous Generation," pp 14-31. (Published in the UK as *Fabulous Science*.)

GAIA Nuclear Power. Lovelock, James. Preface to *Environmentalists for Nuclear Energy* by Bruno Comby. TNR Editions, 1995.

Genetically-Engineered Humans. Barritt, Jason A., *et al.* "Mitochondria in Human Offspring Derived From Ooplasmic Trans-plantation." *Human Reproduction*, 16.3 (2001), pp 513-6. • Email communication from Dr. Joseph Cummins, 4 June 2003. • "First Cases of Human Germline Genetic Modification Announced." *British Medical Journal* 322 (12 May 2001), p 1144. • "Genetically Modified Human Babies?" Australian Broadcasting Corporation, 8 May 2001. • Hawes, S.M., C. Sapienza, and K.E. Latham. "Ooplasmic Donation in Humans: The Potential for Epigenic Modifications." *Human Reproduction* 17.4 (2002), 850-2. • Hill, Amelia. "Horror at 'Three Parent Foetus' Gene Disorders." *Observer* (London), 20 May 2001. • Turner Syndrome Society Website [www.turner-syndrome-us.org].

Insurance Industry. Black, Edwin. *War Against the Weak: Eugenics and America's Campaign to Create a Master Race*. Four Walls Eight Windows, 2003, pp 432-5.

Smoking. The American Council on Science and Health. *Cigarettes: What the Warning Label Doesn't Tell You*. Prometheus Books, 1997.

Bovine Leukemia. Buehring, G.C., K.Y. Choi, and H.M. Jensen. "Bovine Leukemia Virus in Human Breast Tissues." *Breast Cancer Research* 2001 3(Suppl 1):A14. • Buehring, Gertrude, PhD. "Bovine Leukemia Virus Infection and Human Breast Cancer Risk." Grant proposal and final report, 2002. • Kradjian, Robert M., MD. "The Milk Letter: A Message to My Patients." Website of American Fitness Professionals and Associates [www.afpafitness.com], no date. Kradjian is chief of breast surgery, Division of General Surgery, Seton Medical Centre, Daly City, CA. • USDA. "High Prevalence of BLV in US Dairy Herds." Info sheet from the Animal and Plant Health Inspection Service, US Department of Agriculture, undated.

REFERENCES

CAT Scans. Wysong, Pippa. "Doctors Have Little More Info Than Patients About CT Scan Safety." *Medical Post* 39.20 (20 May 2003). • "Computed Tomography Imaging (CT Scan, CAT Scan)" on Imaginis.com.

Medication Errors. Regush, Nicholas. "Medication Errors: Too Little Attention." RedFlagsDaily e-newsletter, 30 May 2003. • Ricks, Delthia. "Poison in Prescription: Illegible Writing Can Lead to Dangerous Medication Errors." *Newsday* (New York), 19 Mar 2001. • Waters, Rob. "Precarious Prescriptions: Can Your Doctor's Handwriting Kill You?" WebMD, 4 Aug 2000. • Website of the United States Pharmacopeial Convention, Inc. [www.usp.org].

Prescription Drugs. Graham, Garthe K., Sidney M. Wolfe, *et al.* "Postmarketing Surveillance and Black Box Warnings." JAMA 288 (2002), pp 955-9. • Lazarou, Jason, M.Sc., Bruce H. Pomeranz, MD, PhD, and Paul N. Corey, PhD. "Incidence of Adverse Drug Reactions in Hospitalized Patients: A Meta-analysis of Prospective Studies." JAMA 279 (1998), pp 1200-5. • Website of the Food and Drug Administration [www.fda.gov]. • Wolfe, Sidney, MD. "Statement by Sidney Wolfe: Recent Events Arguing Against Things Getting Better as Suggested by the FDA Editorial in Tomorrow's JAMA." Public Citizen Website [www.citizen.org], circa 1 May 2002.

Work Kills. International Labor Organization. "Workers' Memorial Day Ceremony to Focus on Emergency Workers, Firefighters." Press release, 24 Apr 2002. • Cullen, Lisa. *A Job to Die For: Why So Many Americans Are Killed, Injured or Made Ill at Work and What to Do About It.* Common Courage Press, 2002. This book uses the following as its sources for the US statistics I've cited: Bureau of Labor Statistics and *Costs of Occupational Injuries and Illnesses* by J. Paul Leigh (University of Michigan Press, 2000).

Elder Suicide. US statistics are for the latest available year (2000) and are from the Centers for Disease Control and Prevention, particularly their Web-based Injury Statistics Query and Reporting System [www.cdc.gov/ncipc/wisqars/] and their factsheet "Suicide in the United States." • Global statistics are from the World Health Organisation's graph: "Distribution of suicide rates (per 100,000), by gender and age, 1998." Located on the WHO's international site [www.who.int].

HIV Tests. Gigerenzer, Gerd. *Calculated Risks: How to Know When Numbers Deceive You.* Simon & Schuster, 2002.

DNA Matching. Gigerenzer, Gerd. *Calculated Risks: How to Know When Numbers Deceive You.* Simon & Schuster, 2002. • Thompson, W.C., F. Taroni, and C.G. Aitken. "How the Probability of a False Positive Affects the Value of DNA Evidence." *Journal of Forensic Sciences* 48.1 (Jan 2003). • Website of L.D. Mueller, professor of biology at the University of California Irvine School of Biological Sciences [darwin.bio.uci.edu/~mueller/]. • Website of *Scientific Testimony*, an online journal devoted to forensic evidence, "edited and published by faculty and students of the Department of Criminology, Law & Society, University of California, Irvine" [www.scientific.org].

Lie Detectors. Opening Statement on Polygraph Screening, by Supervisory Special Agent Dr. Drew C. Richardson, FBI Laboratory Division, before the United States Senate Committee on the Judiciary, Subcommittee on Administrative Oversight and the Courts, Senate Hearing 105-431: A Review of the Federal Bureau of Investigation Laboratory: Beyond the Inspector General Report, 29 Sept 1997. Available at antipolygraph.org.

Bayer. Askwith, Richard. "How Aspirin Turned Hero." *Sunday Times* (London), 13 Sept 1998. • Bogdanich, Walt, and Eric Koli. "2 Paths of Bayer Drug in 80's: Riskier Type Went Overseas." *New York Times*, 22 May 2003. • Metzger, Th. *The Birth of Heroin and the Demonization of the Dope Fiend.* Loompanics Unlimited, 1998.

LSD Therapy. Grof, Stanislav, MD. *LSD Psychotherapy: Exploring the Frontiers of the Hidden Mind.* Hunter House, 1980, 1994. • "Psychedelic Research Around the World" page [www.maps.org/research/] on the Website of the Multidisciplinary Association for Psychedelic Studies. • "LSD: The Drug," Website of the Drug Enforcement Administration [www.usdoj.gov/dea/].

Sagan. Davidson, Keay. *Carl Sagan: A Life.* New York: John Wiley & Sons, 1999. • Grinspoon, Lester. *Marihuana Reconsidered.* Harvard University Press, 1971.

Black Hawk Down. Turner, Megan. "War Film 'Hero' Is a Rapist." *New York Post*, 18 Dec 2001.

SUV Drivers. Bradsher, Keith. *High and Mighty: SUVs—The World's Most Dangerous Vehicles and How They Got That Way.* PublicAffairs (Perseus), 2002, pp 101-7.

"Squaw." Bright, William. "The Sociolinguistics of the 'S-Word': 'Squaw' in American Placenames." Undated article posted to Dr. Bright's Website at the Northern California Indian Development Council [www.ncidc.org/bright/]. • Bruchac, Marge. "Reclaiming the Word 'Squaw' in the Name of the Ancestors." NativeWeb, Nov 1999.

Mailing Letters. Mr. Unzip. *How to Screw the Post Office.* Loompanics Unlimited, 2000.

Advertisers' Influence. Fleetwood, Blake. "The Broken Wall: How Newspapers Are Selling Their Credibility to Advertisers." *Washington Monthly*, Sept 1999. • Kerwin, Ann Marie. "Advertiser Pressure on Newspapers Is Common: Survey." *Editor and Publisher*, 16 Jan 1993. • The Project for Excellence in Journalism. "Local TV News Project – 2002: Investigative Journalism Despite the Odds." On their Website [www.journalism.org].

Art Forgery. Hoving, Thomas. *False Impressions: The Hunt for Big-Time Art Fakes.* Simon & Schuster, 1996. • Nash, Elizabeth. "Was There a Family Conspiracy to Cover up the Truth About Goya's Finest Work?" *Independent* (London), 1 May 2003.

Note: An index for this book is available at books.disinfo.com

Russ Kick is the editor of *Abuse Your Illusions: The Disinformation Guide to Media Mirages and Establishment Lies*; *Everything You Know Is Wrong: The Disinformation Guide to Secrets and Lies*; and *You Are Being Lied To: The Disinformation Guide to Media Distortion, Historical Whitewashes and Cultural Myths*. His upcoming book is *The Disinformation Book of Lists*.

Earlier, he wrote *Outposts: A Catalogue of Rare and Disturbing Alternative Information* and *Psychotropedia: Publications From the Periphery*, as well as editing *Hot Off the Net: Erotica and Other Sex Writings From the Internet*. He has contributed to numerous books, Websites, and periodicals (including the *Village Voice*, which ran his column, "Net-O-Matic").

Russ publishes The Memory Hole [www.thememoryhole.org], devoted to rescuing knowledge and freeing information. His personal Website is Mind Pollen [www.mindpollen.com].